The Computer Time Bomb

How to Keep the Century Date Change From Killing Your Organization

Minda Zetlin

AMA Management Briefing

AMA MEMBERSHIP PUBLICATIONS DIVISION
AMERICAN MANAGEMENT ASSOCIATION

For information on how to order additional copies of this publication, see page 103.

Library of Congress Cataloging-in-Publication Data

Zetlin, Minda.
    The computer time bomb : how to keep the century date change from killing your organization / by Minda Zetlin.
        p.   cm.
    Includes bibliographical references (p.   ).
    ISBN 0-8144-2365-5 (pbk.)
    1. Year 2000 date conversion (Computer systems)   2. Software maintenance.   I. Title.
    QA76.76.S64Z48   1997
    005.1'6—dc21   *97-34031*
                                                                        CIP

Printing number

10   9   8   7   6   5   4   3   2   1

To
Bill,
for the next century

Contents

Acknowledgments

Many people who are in the trenches of the year 2000 battle, and thus have very little time to spare, nevertheless spent a lot of it helping me understand this complex and dangerous phenomenon. Here are a few whose assistance went beyond the call of duty: Irene Dec at Prudential Insurance, who patiently explained many aspects of her company's model year 2000 project; Peter de Jager, consultant and co-author of *Managing 00*, who has a talent for making this problem understandable to nonprogrammers; the Gartner Group, without whose ongoing efforts I never would have learned about Y2K when I did; and research analyst Michael O'Connell, who has shared a store of information. Also, thanks to Bill Ulrich and Ian Hayes, who put together the Software Productivity Group Conference that turned out to be a two-day year 2000 education. As Peter de Jager says: "Go to a year 2000 conference. It will scare you."

And thanks to Martha Peak, former editor of *Management Review*, for recognizing that the year 2000 is indeed a management issue, and for helping to give this book its start.

What Is the
Year 2000 Problem?

The year 2000 problem (also called "Y2K") is the result of a universal programming standard that records dates as six digits (mm/dd/yy) rather than eight, using only two digits for the year. Software that uses two-digit year fields (that is, almost all of it) will understand the year 2000 as "00" if the problem is not corrected in time.

Why Is It Such a Problem?

So some of your dates will look a little funny. What's the big deal?

The big deal is that computers use dates to perform a wide variety of calculations. Inaccurate dates can make them either stop functioning altogether or continue functioning, but inaccurately.

Of these two possibilities, the second is worse. Here are some mishaps that have *already* happened because of the year 2000 problem.

A major company had a simple method for eliminating outdated customer files: The computer would consider the last active year and add five. If the resulting number was smaller than the current year, the file would be automatically deleted.

In 1994, this system worked perfectly. It calculated that 88 plus 5 equaled 93, and since 94 is greater than 93, any accounts that hadn't been active since 1988 were terminated.

In 1995, things began to go awry. When the computer considered accounts that were active in 1995 and added 5, it got not 100 but 00. Is 00 smaller than 95? Of course it is. So the computer deleted those accounts.

By the end of the year, 800 active accounts had been canceled. In 1996, 1,200 more accounts vanished (because 01 is smaller than 96), before the problem was finally caught.

A financial company sold thirty-year annuities to its investors. Because of the thousands of documents and accounts involved, contracts for these annuities were routinely generated by computer and mailed out to customers without human review.

As the computer calculated maturity dates that crossed over from 1999 to 2000, it found a difference of 99 years between the year it saw as "99" and the year it saw as "00." Although that was minus 99 years, many programs do not perceive a difference between negative and positive numbers. Thus, the final values of the annuities were calculated over 129 years instead of 30 years—a difference in value that often reached into the hundreds of thousands of dollars.

Several thousand contracts were automatically sent out before anyone caught the error. That company is now contacting investors, requesting that they rip up the old contracts and sign newly corrected ones instead. For those who refuse, the company will be legally obligated to pay the higher amount.

In a large office building, a maintenance worker accidentally set the elevator computer to the year "00." All the building's elevators settled (gently) to the basement. There they remained until the system was restarted with a correct date. People with offices in that building (and thousands like it) will find themselves climbing to work in January 2000 unless the problem is corrected in time.

Why You Need This Briefing

The worst misconception about the year 2000 problem is that it is primarily a technical problem. This is simply not true. As a technical problem, Y2K is relatively easy. As a management problem, it's an enormous challenge.

Here's an analogy: The building that houses your company burns down and everything inside it is destroyed. Replacing your walls, desks, chairs, telephones, and computers should be easy, from a technical point of view. Keeping your business going during the crisis might be much more difficult. Imagine that the same fire also destroyed your biggest suppliers and customers, and you begin to see the scope of the problem.

Of course, you have insurance, and if a fire did occur, your insurance carrier would help keep your business alive. But consider this: Most insurance companies are now adding riders to their policies that specifically exclude year 2000-related problems from their general coverage.

The year 2000 problem is real; it's not going anywhere. With a little over two years left before December 31, 1999, hopes for "silver bullet" software that will quickly fix the problem are fading. And every organization that uses computers—or even interacts with others that do—will be affected.

Some won't survive. In his report *The Global Economic Impact of the Year 2000 Software Problem*, Capers Jones, chairman of Software Productivity Research, Inc., analyzes the likelihood of business failure due to the year 2000 problem for all U.S. companies. He concludes that very large corporations, most of which have gotten a fairly early start on Y2K (and which have tremendous financial resources), suffer a 1 percent risk of going out of business or declaring bankruptcy because of the year 2000 problem. Small companies, on the other hand, have fewer financial resources, but don't usually own much software. So he puts their risk of year 2000-related failure at 3 percent (though noting that a more significant percentage of small companies will undoubtedly fail for other reasons).

Those numbers are hardly reassuring, but the picture is even grimmer when it comes to midsize companies, which he defines as those with 1,000 to 10,000 employees. Historically, he says, companies this size tend to use a great deal of software but do not necessarily do the proper maintenance on it. He puts the chance of business failure for midsize companies at 5 to 7 percent.

There are about 30,000 companies in the United States that fall into this size range. Thus, Jones notes that if his predictions are correct, up to 2,100 companies could fail because of Y2K. "This is a significant number," he writes, "and it is an open question as to whether the impact of the year 2000 problem is severe enough to trigger a recession." (For more information on Capers Jones's report, see Want to Know More? at the end of this book.)

The time to act is now. This briefing will tell you what every manager needs to know about Y2K, and how to keep it from driving your company under. It will tell you how to approach one of the most difficult project management challenges your company is ever likely to face. It will explain how to avoid some of the legal pitfalls involved. And, though fixing the year 2000 problem is unlikely to be cheap, it will offer some ways to keep the cost to a minimum.

Are You Ready for Y2K? A Self-Test

Do you know if your organization is prepared to deal with the full scope of the year 2000 problem? Unfortunately, many managers who think they have it under control will find out the hard way that Y2K can affect aspects of their business well beyond the information technology (IT) department—and in unexpected ways. By the time this happens, it will probably be too late. Take this quiz and find out how prepared your organization is.

1. Have you performed "triage"—that is, have you determined which of your computer systems are truly needed for your business to survive and which could, if necessary, be allowed to fail?

2. Having determined which tasks are "mission-critical," have you put contingency plans in place for performing these functions without the use of your computers?

3. Have you communicated the importance of this project throughout your organization?

4. Do you have one companywide project manager overseeing the entire year 2000 project? And does this person have the clout within your organization to command the considerable resources necessary for the effort?

5. Have you examined the year 2000 conversion efforts at your essential supplier companies to determine whether they are likely to be completed in time? And if they are not, have you made arrangements to either help with their Y2K efforts or switch to different suppliers if necessary?

6. If your most important customers conduct the same kind of examination at your company, will you pass muster?

7. Have you taken steps to protect yourself from being reinfected with the year 2000 "virus" whenever you receive computer data from outside your company?

8. Have you settled all questions of year 2000 compliance with software suppliers? Established who is responsible for fixing the noncompliant software you already own? Made them legally re-

sponsible for certifying all new software they deliver to you is year 2000-compliant?

9. Have you reviewed all your supplier contracts and included language that makes it clear who is responsible if suppliers fail to meet their delivery schedules or other obligations because of a year 2000 glitch?

10. Speaking of legal documents, have you created a "paper trail" that proves your own top management is seriously concerned with solving this problem?

11. Are you insured against the year 2000 problem? And if so, for how much longer?

12. What will happen to your year 2000 project if a large portion of your programming staff leaves in the middle of it?

13. What will happen to your year 2000 project if the person in charge of it leaves in the middle?

14. Are you considering the year 2000 problem in all relevant areas of your business strategy? (For instance, the question of year 2000 should be part of due diligence for any merger or acquisition deals you conduct in the next three years.)

15. Have you determined on what date your systems will begin to malfunction? For many, many programs, the first failure date is much earlier than January 1, 2000. In fact, systems are malfunctioning already, with errors that may not immediately be recognized as year 2000-related. Do you know when your first failures will occur? And will your mission-critical systems be repaired before then?

The point of this exercise is not so much to learn whether you have the right answers to these questions, but whether you have answers at all. If you have thought about each of these questions, and have taken definite steps toward solving them, then chances are your organization is at least on its way to dealing with its year 2000 problem.

By no means does this questionnaire cover every aspect of Y2K. Even if you have handled every one of these issues, there's no guarantee that your organization is doing everything it needs to. On the other hand, if these questions start you thinking about aspects of the problem that you hadn't yet considered, they'll have served their intended purpose.

1

Management's Biggest Mistake

Not long ago, I met Joe, an information technology (IT) manager for a retail store chain. (Though the name is fictitious, the rest of this story is true.) Retail chains are particularly vulnerable for two reasons: First, they are "high on the food chain"—that is, they sell finished products that must pass through numerous manufacturing operations and other steps, allowing many opportunities for a year 2000-related delay to cause problems. Second, most chains depend on computer systems for such things as inventory control, ordering merchandise, and tracking consumer preferences.

In short, Joe had good reason to be concerned about the year 2000, and the day before we met, he had attended a board of directors meeting at his company. He'd brought a carefully prepared presentation explaining the problems associated with the year 2000 and how he intended to deal with them. But he never got the chance to give it. "The CEO said not to bother with the presentation," Joe recalled. "He said, 'We know we have to do this, so go ahead and do it. How much is it going to cost?'"

Joe gave his estimate of the cost, with a low-end and high-end figure. The CEO responded: "Let's assume you can do it for the lower price. If you need more, let us know." And with that, he sent Joe on his way.

That CEO, I feel certain, believes he acted responsibly in dealing with the year 2000 problem. He gave his information technology manager the funding needed to fix the problem and allowed for the possibility of more if more was needed. What more could an IT manager want?

A lot, it turns out. Here are a few things Joe's board of directors should have thought about.

1. **Sponsorship.** Information technology experts agree that high-level management sponsorship is the make-or-break element in any year 2000 project. Without it, they say, the chances of solving the problem in time are nonexistent.

When I asked Joe what more he wanted from his management, sponsorship was his first answer. In addition to financial resources, the team responsible for a year 2000 project needs the backing of upper management to get priority for its work throughout its company. A year 2000 project that doesn't get that kind of priority is much less likely to be done before systems start to fail.

If the executives at Joe's company were not even willing to take a few minutes to hear about the details of this problem, how could they possibly communicate its importance to the rest of their organization?

2. **Loyalty.** One thing is absolutely certain about every year 2000 fix, whether it is successful or not: It's going to take a long, difficult, miserably unpleasant scramble to get it done. Ed Yourdan, a software engineer and author, describes year 2000 projects as "death march" projects—the kind that keep people up till all hours of the night in a desperate attempt to meet an impossible deadline. At a recent year 2000 conference, he told a conference room full of IT managers to seriously consider quitting their jobs rather than sacrifice their personal lives to such a task.

Indeed, most of them seem pretty mobile already: According to some estimates, the average tenure for a chief information officer (CIO) is three years. And, since two-digit date fields have been around since the earliest days of computer programming, most of these CIOs have inherited, rather than created, the year 2000 problem at their companies.

That being the case, an information technology executive in charge of a year 2000 project might well feel tempted to give up and bail out if an attractive offer arrived from another company. And with more and more companies getting desperate about the year 2000, such offers are multiplying daily. One IT manager at a retail company reported getting an offer to become another company's year 2000 project manager that would have tripled his current pay.

Considering all this, if I were Joe's boss, I would want to make sure he understood how highly his work was valued. Instead, when I talked to him, he was feeling angry and unappreciated.

3. **Liability.** Here's another thing we know about the year 2000 problem: It's going to be the basis for a lot of lawsuits. So much so that law schools around the country are beginning to add special courses on year 2000 liability to their curricula.

One of the defenses in a Y2K case is to show that the officers of the company were fully aware of and concerned about the problem, and did everything in their power to solve it. But what if, because of a year 2000 glitch, Joe's company can't meet its business obligations and finds itself on the defending side of a liability suit? Will the board be able to prove that they were fully aware of and concerned about the problem? Will Joe be able to say under oath that his top management did everything they could?

4. **Strategic decision making.** This is the single most important reason that IT staff cannot handle all elements of fixing a year 2000 problem. Because the year 2000 problem is at least as much a business problem as a technical one, it involves plan-

ning and decision making that have much more to do with business than technology.

"A bank could not justify a year 2000 upgrade of an Assembler system because it was in a marginally profitable leasing division," says William Ulrich, technology consultant, president of the Tactical Strategy Group, and co-author of *The Year 2000 Software Crisis: Challenge of the Century* (see Want to Know More?). "It wasn't a strategic business for the organization, so they opted to sell the division to another company. The bank profited from the sale; the company that bought the division got a new customer base, which is what they were essentially buying. They avoided doing the upgrade because they already had a [year 2000] compliant system. All they had to do was move the data over. So everybody won, and money wasn't spent to fix an outdated system." This was a business decision made by the bank's business managers, not technical staff, he stresses. Clearly, IT staffers are not likely to have the knowledge or clout to recommend such steps as selling a division.

But even if you know in advance that such drastic measures will not be part of your year 2000 solution, some business decisions will have to be made. And they're likely to be highly unpleasant decisions. According to the Gartner Group (a Stamford, Connecticut–based management consulting firm that has done extensive year 2000 research), more than 80 percent of all companies will have some year 2000-related systems failures because they will run out of time to fix all their problems before the year 2000 arrives. Some 30 percent will have failures in mission-critical systems—those that directly impact the companies' survival. "If you really feel your business is ready for the year 2000, and you haven't had some difficult discussions about priorities, then you're not there yet," declares Thomas Klein, a JP Morgan vice president.

"Triage"—a term originally used to describe the process of selecting which wounded soldiers to treat on a battlefield—is commonly used today to refer to the process of deciding which computer systems will be fixed. Is purchasing more important than delivery? Which business functions supersede others? Assuming that some of your systems will fail, which ones will affect your business the least?

Whatever the right answers are to these questions, chances are your information technology staff doesn't have them.

2

What Your IT Department May Be Afraid to Tell You

One of the most surprising things about the year 2000 is how many information technology people—the experts in this field—there are who have been saying that the problem is under control. That it'll all be solved before the year 2000 comes around. Piece of cake.

It doesn't take much research into the year 2000 phenomenon to realize that this optimism is unfounded. Why do so many IT managers sound so upbeat? Basically, there seem to be three reasons: fear, embarrassment, and limited jurisdiction. As a manager, you can't afford to be misled by any of them.

✦ **Fear.** Fear is the easiest of these responses to understand. IT managers report a tendency among top executives to kill the messenger who brings news of a corporate year 2000 problem.

The worst example I've heard concerns Al, the CIO at a major manufacturing company. Al was one of the visionary few who began thinking about the year 2000 problem ten years ago, when it would have been relatively easy to solve. He realized that the most painless way to fix it would be through attrition—

something that would still have been possible back then. As the company's computer systems went through their natural upgrades, each one could be double-checked for year 2000 compliance. By the time the millennium rolled around, the whole company would have its year 2000 problem solved, without enormous hassle or expense.

Al described his concerns about the year 2000 problem, and his suggestions for solving it, to the company's top management. They politely told him he was out of his mind. In the mid-1980s, nobody had ever heard of the year 2000 problem. If they had, they thought what many people still think today: *Way before the deadline comes, software vendors will have invented some magic fix to prevent the 00 date from causing trouble.* In any case, how could they worry about an uncertain problem ten years in the future when they had serious concerns that demanded immediate attention?

Al kept after them, reminding them of the danger, voicing his concerns at every executive session he attended. Eventually, he became so much of an annoyance that he was fired. At the time, he thought his career had been derailed forever. Today, he runs a successful year 2000 consulting firm. Present-day executives who want to know why corporate technology people didn't start dealing with the year 2000 problem earlier should keep Al's story in mind.

But there's another lesson here: Technology people have good cause to downplay the severity of the problem. "IT people have known about this for years," notes Vinny Mullineaux, president of Millennia III, a professional services company that specializes in the year 2000 problem. "It's the business community that hasn't known about it. People are traditionally unwilling to promote bad news up the ladder. So there's an information block between CIOs and top executives."

✦ **Embarrassment.** But if fear of retribution is one factor that might encourage computer experts to downplay the year 2000 problem, there's another: plain, garden-variety embarrassment. "To convince management that it's really as bad as we know it to be, we must first convince them that we really could have been that stupid," says Peter de Jager, an Ontario-based consultant who has been working for years to bring Y2K to world attention, and who has gained an international reputation as a year 2000 authority.

"Just put yourself in the shoes of the IT person who has to say to his or her boss: 'You know all that stuff I wrote for that salary you're paying me? None of it will work after 1999.' "

✦ **Limited jurisdiction.** Another reason for your technology staff to worry less—and you to worry more—is that not all aspects of the year 2000 problem necessarily fall within their domain. Chances are, your IT staff is mostly concerned with fixing outdated programs, older programs written in languages like COBOL and FORTRAN, on your company's mainframe computer. Updating these will be difficult enough, but that's only part of the solution.

Throughout your company, there are personal computers (PCs) sitting on people's desks. The people who use them can easily create applications such as spreadsheets on these desktops without your IT department's even knowing. There are client/server systems and local area networks (LANs) linking these PCs together, which may also fall outside your information technology department's jurisdiction. Chances are, your IT people will consider their year 2000 work done without ever giving much thought to these PC networks.

In fact, that might be a natural thing for them to do. Conventional wisdom in the computer industry is that since personal computers and client/server systems are newer products than mainframes, they are unlikely to suffer from the year 2000 problem. But conventional wisdom is wrong.

Ian Hayes, head of Clarity Consulting (in Marblehead, Massachusetts) and co-author of *The Year 2000 Software Crisis*, has examined client/server systems at dozens of companies, and says he has yet to find one that is year 2000-ready. Hayes, who specializes in strategic consulting, has also predicted that the greatest year 2000 business failure will not result from a computer crash. Instead, he says, it will be a disastrous financial decision based on information from a faulty spreadsheet. If so, it'll be a danger the company's information technology staff may never even have considered.

An Overwhelming Project

Even if they limit themselves to mainframe programs, many information technology departments will find that the year 2000 problem is more than they can handle. The very nature of the problem itself makes it perplexing to solve.

The first step in a year 2000 software fix is to find those parts of the program that refer to dates. It sounds simple enough, and it would be simple enough—if one could walk up to a mainframe and ask it which lines of programming "code" contain date fields. Unfortunately, one can't. And there isn't any obvious way to tell which fields in a program might be dates.

To understand the severity of this problem, it helps to know a little bit about how programmers work. A program—anything from a computer game to a word processor—is nothing more than a collection of instructions. The programmers who write the instructions usually believe they themselves will be the only ones to see them. So, when they name a date field (a part of the program where a date will be entered) there's no real need to give it a clearly understandable name like "date." Programmers can, and have, named date fields after everything from their boyfriend or girlfriend to their favorite baseball player.

If the programs are a few years old, the person who wrote them has most likely moved on to another company or even retired. That leaves it to those given the job of fixing the year 2000 problem to sort through the lines of programming left behind, and to try and figure out which fields involve dates.

That's bad enough, but it gets worse if you consider the

problem of lost "source code." Source code is the actual programming instructions the programmer wrote in COBOL, FOR-
TRAN, UNIX, or some other programming language, which is
then automatically translated into "machine code" that runs on
the actual computer. To the human eye, machine code looks like
this:

00000780	C088D503	6038C100	07725810	C05C07F1
00000790	5800C084	5000D260	5810C07C	07F15800
000007A0	D2385000	D260D203	6104C0EC	41106030
000007B0	5010D278	41106091	5010D27C	9680D27C

Machine code is all that's needed for a program to work
perfectly well. But even an accomplished programmer can't tell
by looking what these instructions say, let alone whether they
involve dates. And, in some cases where the original programmer has moved on, the source code is nowhere to be found.

Missing source code is a surprisingly common problem.
Most companies with any history of computer use can't find at
least some of their source code; for some, the problem may ex-
tend to 25 percent of their software. Overall, the Gartner Group
estimates that about 10 percent of the world's software has missing source code.

To make sure their year 2000 problem is solved, these organizations face an unpleasant choice: They must either jettison
the existing programs and write new ones or hire a vendor to
reconstruct the source code from machine code, a difficult process. Either way, the fix is expensive and time-consuming.

Last, there's the interconnected nature of today's computers. Few computers today operate in a vacuum. Just as the
world's businesses are becoming more networked and interdependent, so are the world's computers. Massive amounts of information, much of it containing dates, are passed among them
each day.

So even a company that has managed the difficult task of
converting all its own software to four-digit years will still face

trouble in the likely event that its computers receive information from outside that uses two-digit year fields.

This is why the year 2000 problem is sometimes called the "millennium virus." As with a computer virus, there's a risk of contamination every time your computer accepts data from an external source.

Now for the Biggest Part of the Job

All of the above is hard enough. But what I've described so far is less than half the effort involved in a typical Y2K system fix. "The investigation stage makes up about 15 to 20 percent of the actual work," says Abe Lichtig, technical specialist in the information resources department at Consolidated Edison (Con Ed), New York City's gas and electric utility. "Modifying the programs is about another 15 to 20 percent.

"The real effort is testing the system. It's relatively easy to identify where dates are, and make a determination of what you need to do about them. But then you have to fool the system into thinking it's the year 2000, and then literally test every single program and every application."

This testing stage is the most labor-intensive part of the project. It's one reason many companies like Con Ed are outsourcing a lot of the work to vendors who use programmers in places like India and Eastern Europe to handle part of the workload. According to Peter de Jager, the year 2000 problem has brought new legitimacy to the offshore software development industry. "The reality is, we don't have enough people over here to do the job," he says.

A different, and more serious, problem arises when you consider the shortage of qualified programmers who can handle the more technical aspects of the conversion. The year 2000 problem is a major software overhaul that nearly every organization in the world must undertake—and they're all doing it at the same time. It's easy to see why this situation would create an

excessive demand for programmers, a demand the programmers themselves can easily recognize as a temporary opportunity they should take advantage of while they can.

And they are. Stories abound within the industry of older
programmers returning from retirement for huge salaries; of
younger programmers demanding and getting $400 an hour or
more; of desperate companies luring programmers away from
each other with ever more lucrative deals.

Y2K demands some special strategies in the human resources (HR) area, and these will be discussed more fully in
Chapter 7. The important point to consider now is that an IT
department that thinks it has the year 2000 problem under control may not have factored the likely defection of key personnel
into its plans.

The Year 2000 Problem Is Really
the Year 1999 Problem

What's the latest deadline for solving your organization's year
2000 problem? December 31, 1998. That's right: 1998, *not* 1999.

Why the rush? For two good reasons. The first is that even
after your company's year 2000 solution has been carefully assessed, implemented, and tested, chances are your newly compliant software will contain some bugs. Bugs are pretty much
inevitable in new or upgraded software of any complexity what-
soever. This fact is so widely recognized by the computer industry that software developers routinely distribute "beta test"
copies of new or upgraded software to thousands of selected
users months before releasing it to the general public. And computer experts commonly avoid buying the first version of any
new software since they know for a certainty that it will contain
bugs. Considering all that, it's simple prudence to have a year in
which programs can be tested by users before the actual year
2000 deadline hits.

But there's a second, even better reason for you to get the job done by 1998: The year setting "99" will also likely cause your programs to misbehave in surprising ways. "You see, the same programmers, designers and developers who didn't think their systems would still be in use in the year 2000 also did not believe those same systems would still be in use in the year 1999," explains year 2000 consultant Warren S. Reid in an article on his World Wide Web page. (See Want to Know More? at the end of this briefing.)

Thus, he says, they deliberately programmed the year setting "99" to have a special meaning. What that meaning was varies from program to program. In some cases, it might mean "end of input"; in others, it means "delete this record." Whatever it is, chances are you'll find out the hard way if your year 2000 work is unfinished in 1999. "September 9, 1999 [in other words: "9/9/99"] is one of the scariest dates we have coming," comments JP Morgan's Thomas Klein. "In many programs, that will function as a red flag."

Keep in mind that 1998 is the latest possible deadline, not the earliest. If your software considers dates in the future at all (payment schedules, maintenance schedules, expiration dates, etc.), you could start experiencing year 2000-related glitches a lot earlier.

Many companies have. Long-term observers of the year 2000 industry should recall that real concern about this issue, and the real market for year 2000 solutions, came into existence around the beginning of 1995. According to Gartner Group research analyst Michael O'Connell, this timing is no accident. "A lot of applications have five-year projections and they started running into trouble," he notes. "That's when people started realizing that this was a real problem."

As the year 2000 draws closer, more and more of these forward-looking applications will start giving faulty data. Unfortunately, most IT managers have set their sights on December 1998 as the final deadline (a big enough challenge) without considering what malfunctions might occur in the meantime. The result is that some organizations that are right on schedule with their year 2000 fix will still experience system failures over the next year.

On Time? An Unimpressive Record

Think back to the last computer project you were involved with. Your IT department set up your new equipment or software within budget and right on schedule. You flipped the switch, started the program, and everything worked perfectly. No one using the new system had any trouble at all making it work.

If this is an accurate description, then your company is highly unusual—and very, very lucky. For most information technology projects, the norm is quite different. "What would most managers consider to be an acceptable business risk of failure?" de Jager asks. "Is 5 percent high? Is 10 percent?

"In the computer industry, our failure rate for delivering something on time is more than 80 percent. That's a well-known fact in our industry."

I've repeated this statistic to computer industry experts, and a few have disputed it. But only to say that it's too generous: Computer projects are actually finished on schedule *less* than 20 percent of the time. Indeed, according to one estimate, at least 96 percent of the time, computer people either deliver a project late or cut back on the project itself to get it in on time.

Does this mean computer people are lazy, dishonest, or incapable of proper time management? Not at all. It has to do with the nature of computers and computer programs themselves. Something unexpected almost always goes wrong, and it's practically impossible to predict when it will go right.

When I took my one and only serious programming course in college, I always finished my assignments with twenty-four hours to spare, sometimes staying up half the night to get them done. It's not that I was seeking to punish myself or experiment with sleep deprivation. It's just I could never actually predict when I would be finished with a program until the moment when I popped it in the computer and—surprise!—it executed correctly. Rather than risk being late, I'd actually get things done the day before they were due. (I was one of the few who did well in that class, but my other grades suffered because of it.)

Life is not much different for today's corporate technology people, except that they don't have scholastic vacations in which to recover from staying up all night or other classes to ignore while they work on software.

"As IT people, we're a very honest group when dealing with other people, but we do have a tendency to lie to ourselves about our ability to deliver," Ulrich says. "We've all worked with people who would gladly work till four in the morning to make a deadline. And a lot of people will be working till four in the morning on a regular basis to address this issue. But at some point you burn out and you can't continue working those hours."

The Project Analogy

Ulrich has done research comparing the year 2000 fix to other, more typical software conversion projects. For a company with 50 million lines of computer code (that is, a medium-size company), if the IT department began "aggressively" converting code at the beginning of 1997 in order to be done by 1999, it would have to deliver the equivalent of twelve fully tested, fully implemented software conversion projects per quarter for eight consecutive quarters. At a company with 75 million lines of code, the IT department would have to deliver the equivalent of twenty projects per quarter. With 100 million lines of code, it goes up to twenty-five projects per quarter. And many companies have much, much more.

"Now, most of us don't do that," Ulrich says. "Most of us don't deliver that many conversion projects in any quarter, let alone eight consecutive quarters, without missing a deadline.

We're up against the wall in terms of being able to deliver these things, from a dollar standpoint, a resource standpoint, and from a sheer production standpoint.

"I don't know how many CIOs have looked at these numbers and said, 'That's going to be hard to do!' But it is going to be hard to do."

The Myth of the Silver Bullet

"Oh, they'll come up with *something!*" This is a comment I've heard over and over from people who feel certain that the software developers of the world cannot fail to invent some automatic solution to the year 2000 problem. After all, it would be the money-making opportunity of a lifetime.

This imaginary piece of software is what the computer industry calls a "silver bullet," a sort of smart bomb that will wend its way through your programs, identify all the lines with potential year 2000 problems, and automatically correct them without human aid. Something, as one programmer put it, that you can "pop in on Friday, and when you get to work Monday, it's all done."

There's no denying that a software company that created such a tool would reap huge financial rewards. Some have already made claims to have created silver bullets. And though the term "fully automated" has been used somewhat creatively in this context, there are many software tools that make the job easier and more efficient.

But if there ever was hope of a genuine silver bullet with which to shoot down the year 2000 problem, that hope is disappearing fast. There are literally thousands of ways that programmers store and use dates within computer programs. No one piece of software could find them all—even if it was limited to just one computer language such as COBOL.

And at this point, chances are no one is even trying that hard. The year 2000 problem presents a business opportunity of limited duration, something the world's software vendors are well aware of. By early 1997, most year 2000 vendors had switched the bulk of their budgets away from research and development (R&D) in favor of marketing and sales. Their logic was simple: If they did not start aggressively selling the solutions they had developed, they would miss their only chance to make money in this market.

Charles Phillips and William Farrell, Morgan Stanley computer industry analysts, identified this trend in March 1997 in a special white paper on investing in Y2K. (See Want to Know More? at the end of this briefing.) In their view, that meant the chances of a silver bullet appearing were now "next to nil."

Nonetheless, hope for the silver bullet has prompted leaders of both industry and government to take a "wait and see" approach, rather than diving right in with a costly year 2000 fix. The problem is that there won't be much to see. And, whatever they do, they can't afford to wait.

3

The Big Picture

It's January 2000. There's no food in the refrigerator, but you're not sure you can get to the local grocery store. None of the traffic lights in your town are working—for that matter, neither is your car (which is controlled by a dashboard computer). You can't use your credit cards to pay for the groceries or your ATM card to get cash. A run on your bank has put it on the verge of collapse, and in any case, it has no record that an account in your name ever existed. On the bright side, you're not planning to pay any income tax.

In the past few weeks, there have been several airplane crashes and one nuclear accident, but you don't know anything about them: Your television and radio aren't working.

Outside, you hear shouting. None of the welfare recipients in your city have received their checks, and they're growing increasingly restive. You pick up the phone to dial 911. But, of course, there's no dial tone.

This doomsday scenario was brought to you courtesy of a variety of year 2000 pundits whose job it is to imagine the worst that could happen. Will all these disasters take place at once? Probably not. But any of them could if the systems involved aren't made compliant in time.

In all seriousness, many year 2000 experts recommend precautions that include canceling any flights planned during the first six months of 2000 (since both air traffic control and airline maintenance schedules depend on computers) and keeping every receipt for every transaction you make during 1999 (to create a paper trail and to prove that you exist, in case you start disappearing from computer records).

Whether you follow these suggestions or not, keep this in mind: The effect of Y2K will be felt well outside your company and even your business community. You and your employees will likely be affected in your personal lives as well.

Governments Want More Time

One area of special concern is government. The federal government is notoriously unprepared for the year 2000. The authors of the Morgan Stanley white paper (see Want to Know More?) explain the reason succinctly:

> Everyone asks why companies waited so long to fix their computer date problems when they knew about it years ago. The answers, we would suggest, are that companies are focused on a 2–3 year investment cycle and that it's difficult to ask for buckets of money for a nonproductive expense until productivity becomes an issue. Arguably, that kind of reasoning has brought corporate America to the brink of year 2000. But what if your investment horizon were only one year and you weren't concerned about productivity at all, in fact you had actually shut down operations because you couldn't decide on a full year's budget? Well then, you'd be the government, and you'd be in deep trouble!

The report goes on to note that when Congress surveyed twenty-four federal agencies in April 1996 to determine their readiness for Y2K, the results were highly unimpressive. Only six agencies had even gotten so far as to create an estimate of what achieving compliance would cost them. Four had not even begun to address the issue. And one, the Department of Transportation, was so disorganized that it could not even answer the survey, according to Virginia Congressman Tom Davis.

Year 2000 watchers everywhere have high hopes of failure at the Internal Revenue Service (IRS), an agency with a particularly gruesome Y2K problem. In June 1997, IRS CIO Arthur Gross told the audience at an industry gathering that the agency was struggling with the task of modernizing its computer systems and tracking down its date fields at the same time. Further complicating matters are the 19 million tax returns submitted each year either electronically or by the phone-based TeleFile system. This makes for a great deal of third-party data exchange.

The official line was still that the IRS would deal with the year 2000 problem in time. But year 2000 observers continue to speculate. They note that the agency has some of the most date-intensive software on the planet. What's more, it is already saddled with multiple layers of reprogramming created as tax laws changed from year to year. The probable result is "spaghetti code"—complex calculations that have no clear beginning or end. Because of all this, some year 2000 analysts have predicted that Y2K will bring about what Steve Forbes could not: passage of a flat tax.

Overall, President Clinton has proposed $2.3 billion for the federal year 2000 conversion project in the fiscal 1998 budget. But most experts predict that the cost of the fix will be much higher, perhaps as high as $30 billion.

Taken together, federal, state, and local governments in the United States and abroad are the most unpredictable piece in the year 2000 puzzle. According to Gartner Group's Michael O'Connell, this is the reason that the company's projections of worldwide year 2000 costs range from $300 billion to $600 billion. "We've had a difficult time quantifying the potential implications within governments," he explains. "The low end [projected total expense for all governments worldwide] is $20 billion, but the high end is $250 to $300 billion."

If accurate projections are hard to come by, some broad generalizations are still possible. For example, experts agree that, however late the world's businesses are in tackling the year 2000 problem, the world's governments (U.S. federal government included) are later still. And, though levels of preparedness vary widely, state and local governments in the United States appear to be slightly ahead of their federal counterparts. (For instance, Nebraska has already instituted a two-cent-a-pack cigarette tax to help pay for its year 2000 conversion.)

On the other hand, governments of countries outside the United States are generally less prepared than the U.S. federal government. By the same token, most foreign companies have been slower to address the problem than American ones, and these two facts have combined to cause international business executives some serious concern. They note that Japan, for example, seems to have done little to address the problem, even though studies show that the country will need some 200,000 more IT professionals than it has.

Meanwhile, in Europe, the planned introduction of an international currency (called EMU for European Monetary Unit) is arriving at the same time as the year 2000 problem, by an unfortunate coincidence. This means European businesses and governments will need to perform two major software conversion projects simultaneously.

Plan for Failure

The evidence is clear that there are likely to be at least some Y2K-related failures of government computer systems at the federal, state, and local levels, as well as abroad. One huge difference between most governments and most companies is that governments are responsible for many more systems whose operations are literally a matter of life and death (airplane traffic, dam and bridge maintenance, police deployment and payroll, to name just a few). Obviously, these systems will gain priority as the truly mission-critical repairs they are. Others, such as procurement and accounts payable, will likely fall behind.

What if your company is dependent on the government for either income or data? What steps should you take? Your options are depressingly few. As one year 2000 consultant put it, "We can say to a vendor, 'Hey, you need to be compliant. If you don't get your act together, we're going to change vendors.' But we can't say, 'Hey, we're going to change governments.'"

By the same token, with a private supplier you might be able to stipulate year 2000 compliance in your purchase agreements, leaving you the option of suing for breach of contract if it fails to deliver as promised because of Y2K. However, where the government is concerned, even if you have grounds for a suit, your legal remedies are, as lawyers say, limited.

That being the case, it's a good idea to pay particular attention to your relationships with government-business contacts. Use them to find out exactly how much disruption your company is likely to experience and to lobby for a sufficient Y2K budget. Needless to say, you'll want to ask some detailed questions if you're met with blanket assurances that everything is under control.

Beyond that, the best precaution you can take is to prepare for the worst. If the government is an important source of revenue for your organization, try to focus on other areas or prepare for some disruption. If you depend on receiving information or material from government sources, now's the time to look for backup sources.

Your options widen a little when dealing with state and local governments, and with the governments of some foreign countries. Depending on your relationship and your resources, you may even consider offering your help to get a local government up to speed. Millennia III, for instance, is offering its consulting services for free to the town of Westport, Connecticut, where it is headquartered.

Depending on the size of your organization, you may also have some leverage. If a local government is dragging its feet, and your business is an important element of the local economy, the fear that you could relocate may finally inspire it to take the issue of year 2000 compliance seriously.

4

How Could They Let This Happen?

It would be just like programmers to shorten "the year 2000 problem" to "Y2K"—exactly the kind of thinking that created this situation in the first place!

—Source unknown

If you're a manager faced with the year 2000 problem—and with spending huge sums on a project whose only benefit will be that you continue operating as before—you're probably having a very natural reaction. You're mad as hell and looking for someone to blame. And it looks like there *is* someone to blame: those nameless, faceless programmers who created the two-digit year field in the early days of computing. Didn't they know the millennium was coming? Why did they do this to us?

As it turns out, they had very good reasons. For those of us who've accepted the World Wide Web as a fact of daily life, it can be difficult to remember how dramatically computers have changed in a remarkably short time.

But they have. Twenty years ago, when this industry was in its infancy, many programmers still entered data into computers on Hollerith cards—hole-punched cards with eighty columns of characters each. Even computers that had evolved to use keyboards for data entry often operated on "virtual cards" using the same eighty-column format.

Whether one was using keyboards or cards, one thing remained constant: Memory storage space was precious, both monetarily and as a corporate resource. One megabyte of storage cost more than $2,000 in 1963, and more than $400 in 1972. It costs about a dollar today. (Please note that what I am referring to here is memory storage, usually on disk, *not* the megabytes of random access memory [RAM] many personal computer users are adding to make their machines function more powerfully.)

Thus, if looked at from a historical viewpoint, the programming practice that created Y2K actually showed sound business judgment. In an article in the inaugural issue of the *Year/2000 Journal* (see Want to Know More?), consultants Leon Kappelman and Phil Scott estimate that companies have saved between $1.2 and $2 million per gigabyte (1,000 megabytes) of storage since 1963. Even ten and fifteen years ago, many companies had hundreds of gigabytes of information stored, so it's easy to see that the accrued savings have been huge—even when compared with the cost of the year 2000 conversion these companies must now implement.

Savings or not, most programmers who worked in the 1960s and 1970s recall that using four-digit year fields then would have been out of the question. "It was tough getting things to fit on machines as every byte was precious," recalls one. "Putting '19' in a date could have gotten you fired."

Others remember asking their bosses what would happen to the two-digit years when the millennium rolled over. The response was usually a laugh or a comment about crossing that bridge when we come to it—or that "we'll all be retired by then, anyway!"

That may sound uncaring, but there was also a more serious answer. Programmers in those days expected the systems they were working on to be in operation for about five to ten years.

By the time the millennium arrived, they were quite certain these systems would be obsolete, so the two-digit year would have no actual effect. This was not an unreasonable expectation. Software evolves very fast, so fast that even Windows 95 is soon to be replaced with something new after less than two years on the market.

What no one expected is how older "legacy" systems could and would be upgraded, reconfigured, and refurbished so that their basic software and databases could survive over decades, improved but never actually replaced. This is also the explanation for a very odd phenomenon: Even though COBOL is an ancient computer language that hasn't been taught in colleges for several years, far more of it is in use on corporate and institutional computers than anything else. In fact, the Gartner Group estimates that as of 1994, there were about 250 billion lines of code in corporate software portfolios worldwide, and about 180 billion of them were COBOL.

Out With the Old Problem, In With the New Problem

But there's another problem at work here, one that *can* justly be blamed on unthinking programmers: the practice of lifting existing software routines—two-digit years and all—and dropping them into present-day programming. That's right: *There are computer programs being written in 1997 that are not year 2000-compliant.*

Find that hard to believe? So did I when I first heard about it. I was so astounded that I posted a question about it on an online computer programming message board. One COBOL programmer wrote back: "I must admit, I just completed a major development effort in which we set a four-digit year standard for the code in the application, and some two-digit year code still slipped through, specifically related to calendar quarter designations." He added, perhaps unnecessarily: "Rigid quality assurance review in this area is needed for programs being written today."

It's not that programmers are lazy or careless. But modern programs have so many thousands of lines of code in them that to create each one from scratch would be hopelessly inefficient and prohibitively expensive. So programmers really have no choice but to lift sections of software from existing programs, some of which are not year 2000-compliant.

Careful programmers may catch some of these errors, but they don't always. It is thus an extremely common occurrence for organizations today to find themselves installing newly developed software that will malfunction in the year 2000. Often these are complex, powerful new programs that took months or even years to develop.

What this means for your company is that solving the year 2000 problem may be something like painting the Golden Gate Bridge—by the time you get to the end, you have to start at the beginning again. But while painting the bridge may make sense as a permanently ongoing project, your year 2000 conversion project is something you have to finish, or risk real consequences to your organization.

So it's essential that you stop the cycle. The only way to do that is by subjecting every piece of new software to stringent year 2000 testing before it's installed on any of your company's computers. This applies not only to software developed inhouse, but also to programs purchased from vendors. In fact, one IT manager who's been burned by new, supposedly year 2000-compliant software that actually wasn't advocates such testing even for off-the-shelf software. After all, software vendors' programmers reuse preexisting software, too.

5

How Much Will It Cost?

Discussions of the expense involved in fixing the year 2000 problem always involve numbers that boggle the mind. According to Capers Jones's *Global Economic Impact* report (see Want to Know More? Recommended Other Reading), Y2K will be one of the most expensive problems humankind has ever faced. As I noted in Chapter 3, the Gartner Group's projection for total worldwide costs to solve the year 2000 problem is $300 to $600 billion. But some experts believe even these figures are conservative, and other projections go as high as $1.5 *trillion*.

In fact, it's impossible to predict exactly how much it will cost. For one thing, expenses for hiring both programmers and year 2000 consultants are rising rapidly as the supply of available expertise diminishes, and companies scramble to sign up whomever they can. Furthermore, most organizations and governments still do not have a complete grasp of what changes they will need to make to achieve year 2000 compliance, or exactly how they will carry out those changes.

All this makes it difficult to predict what the final cost of Y2K will be, though it's worth noting that most early estimates have been revised upward as the millennium approaches. Since the United States is the most computerized country on earth, American government and businesses will be spending a disproportionately large share of that money.

What does all this mean to your organization? Well, for one thing, fixing the year 2000 problem won't be cheap. And no matter how reasonable your Y2K budget may seem, be prepared for the possibility that you might have to spend more.

$1.50 a Line

Most cost estimates for year 2000 fixes today are based on the number of lines of code your organization uses. These usually refer to programming in use that was written or customized specifically for your organization, and that runs on a mainframe.

Even a relatively small company, if it's been around for a few years and uses a mainframe for any of its functions, is likely to have several million lines of code. In large and even medium-size organizations, 100 million lines of code or more are not uncommon.

Until about a year ago, estimates for fixing a company's year 2000 problem usually used a standard $1 per line of code. But as the cost of hiring the necessary expertise grows, estimates for software repair are growing as well. By late 1996, the Gartner Group was using a standard of $1.10 per line in its predictions. In March 1997, Morgan Stanley's white paper (see Want to Know More?) claimed that $1.50 a line represented an industry standard. By the time this briefing appears, the industry norm may well have risen higher.

And That's Not All

I must stress that this $1.10 or $1.50 a line refers to a very specific part of an organization's year 2000 project: finding, correcting, and testing software that has been written or customized for the company and that runs on its mainframe. While this may well prove to be the biggest portion of the expense involved in deal-

ing with Y2K, it is by no means all of it. A company will probably also have to pay for:

+ Repair or replacement of personal computers, client/
  server systems, and related software that are not year
  2000-compliant
+ Upgrading of off-the-shelf software that is not year 2000-
  compliant
+ Business problems associated with the year 2000 (for instance, you may have to switch suppliers or keep a
  greater inventory because of potential year 2000 problems at your supplier companies)
+ Extra clerical and staff time as workers take over computer tasks (such as invoicing) that were not corrected in
  time
+ Special year 2000 insurance
+ Litigation relating to year 2000 snafus

That said, there are certain issues that can make your year
2000 repair especially costly. Ask yourself the following questions.

+ **Are you starting late?** There are many, many reasons to
undertake a year 2000 repair earlier rather than later. One of
them is that it will cost less. The closer you get to the deadline,
the more you will have to pay, both for in-house programming
work and for outside vendors to help with the problem. Indeed,
as this briefing goes to press, the demand for these qualified
experts is so high that you may have trouble hiring them at all.
If your Y2K fix is already well under way, chances are that you'll
wind up paying less for it.

+ **Have you recently been through a merger or acquisition?** At United Healthcare (based in Hartford, Connecticut), a
well-organized IT department started its year 2000 project in
plenty of time for the new millennium. The company determined that it had 120 million lines of code in its inventory. Be-

cause the IT department got an early start, and because it was able to take advantage of economies of scale, the IT department projected a cost of only $80 million for its millennium project.

All was going well until early 1997, when United Healthcare announced it had acquired the American Association of Retired Persons' (AARP) Medicare supplement insurance business. From an insurance industry point of view, this was a huge coup. From a Y2K point of view, it created a huge challenge. At this writing, United Healthcare's IT staff was still assessing the year 2000 problem for the new AARP portion of its project. But because it will be starting much later, fixing the AARP year 2000 problem may well cost more per line of code than the original United Healthcare project did.

✦ **How common are your company's computers and systems?** The more widely used your systems are, the easier it will be to find programmers with the expertise to fix them. Thus, IBM mainframes, IBM-type personal computers, Apple computers, and DOS- and UNIX-based systems should be fairly straightforward to repair or upgrade with year 2000-compliant software provided by vendors.

You're likely to have a bigger problem if your computer systems are highly unusual, if they were specifically built for your industry or company, or if you're working in programs written in more specialized languages. You may also have trouble if you're working with "orphan" hardware or software made by a company that has since gone out of business. Any of these factors can increase the difficulty and substantially raise the cost of a year 2000 repair.

✦ **How much lost source code does your company have?** In Chapter 2, I discussed the problem of missing source code (cases where the original human-written program is lost, and only the machine code, which runs on the actual computer but is incomprehensible to a human, remains).

The Gartner Group estimates that 10 percent of the programming currently in use worldwide has missing source code.

If your company has had its own in-house software for five years or more, chances are some of your source code is among the missing. An organization faced with missing source code has two unpleasant choices: either undertake a source code recovery project—an expensive and time-consuming job that must be completed before the program can even be assessed for year 2000 compliance—or write a new program from scratch to do what the old one did.

Writing a new program will probably take even longer than doing source code recovery on the old one. In this case, the missing source code will present a different problem. Without a legible copy of the original program available, it will be difficult for new programmers to determine in complete detail exactly what the old program did. For instance, they may know that a piece of software tracks accounts payable and automatically invoices customers, but they may not realize that the same program also interacts with other company systems to block delivery of product if an account is sixty days late, or sends the information to a collection agency after a further delay. These tasks could wind up being left out of the rewritten program.

Also, as noted in Chapter 4, many new programming projects being completed today are still not year 2000-compliant—sometimes despite their programmers' best intentions. This means that if you choose to re-create rather than recover a program with lost source code, the new software will still need to be stringently tested for year 2000 compliance before it can be used.

Getting Costs Under Control

Fixing the year 2000 problem is an expensive project your company can't afford not to do. But this does not mean that you have no choice at all about how much you spend to do it. As is often the case, however, a less expensive solution may also be a less perfect, or less permanent, solution. Here are some cost-cutting steps you can take.

✦ **Severe triage.** One obvious way to cut the cost of fixing a system is not to fix it at all. This is clearly not a decision you can make in every case. But, as we have seen, it's a virtual certainty that some of your organization's systems will not be repaired in time, no matter how much you spend.

So it's a good idea to make cost-cutting part of the equation when you consider what to fix and what to leave. Some problems (like the disappearing accounts described in What Is the Year 2000 Problem?) will fix themselves in a few years, as the computer stops trying to make calculations that cross over the 00/99 threshold. Other systems, such as payroll, can readily be outsourced, and doing so might be less costly than fixing them. In still other cases, you may decide that a date of "1900" rather than "2000" on an internal document is something you can live with.

✦ **The two-digit fix.** As the business technology community struggles with the year 2000 problem, four-digit years are becoming a standard for data that are transferred among companies. Given the patchwork of variations in year 2000 solutions from company to company, this development is probably a very good thing. It does not, however, dictate what goes on inside your company's computer.

At the programming level, there are two ways to correct a year 2000 problem. One is to rewrite the program so that the year is represented by a four-digit field instead of a two-digit field. This means profoundly changing the program, and although it is the clearest and most permanent solution to a year 2000 problem, it is also the most expensive.

Another possible solution exists, and though it is "quick and dirty" (as programmers say), it is a lot less costly. That solution is to insert an "if . . . then" statement into the program that allows it to keep using two-digit year fields and to make an educated guess as to which century they refer to.

It works like this. Let's say your company has been in business for sixty years and is dealing with thirty-year mortgages. In no case will your software ever have to look more than sixty years into the past, or thirty years into the future. Thus, the earliest year that could exist on your system is 1938, and the latest is 2028.

If that was the case, you could insert a simple equation into this program to convert two-digit years to four-digit years: "If nn [two-digit year] is equal to or greater than 38, then nn equals 19nn. If nn is less than 38, then nn equals 20nn." When software developers refer to "windowing," "procedural," or "interpretation" year 2000 changes, this is what they mean.

It is much less expensive, and possibly quicker, than replacing two-digit fields with four-digit fields. In fact, according to the Gartner Group, while the approximate cost for a two-digit solution is $1.10 per line of code, it's $1.65 per line of code for "field expansion," the four-digit fix. Not surprisingly, Gartner has also found that some 80 percent of the companies it's tracking are opting for the two-digit solution, at least in some of their systems.

The two-digit solution does have obvious drawbacks, however. First of all, it can only be applied in some cases. A database that includes the years houses were built, for example, could not guess in 2002 whether "02" meant 1902 or 2002. Second, it is not a permanent solution. In the mortgage example above, the fix would stop working in 2008 when the company begins writing mortgages that reach into 2038.

Of course, 2008 is a decade away. Both hardware and software are developing so rapidly that there's a good chance the mortgage software will be either obsolete or easily upgraded by the time the 2038 date is needed. In any case, there's plenty of time to worry about it before then. On the other hand, it was thinking like this that created the year 2000 problem in the first place.

✦ **Elimination of "dead" code.** Strange as it sounds, as programs are reconfigured and rewritten, parts of them remain in the system after they no longer have any practical application. Missing source code adds to the cost of a year 2000 project because it must be recovered or replaced before the Y2K fix can go forward. Conversely, dead code wastes money because, although the code exists, it no longer has any useful application. Although it will add another project to your year 2000 fix, you can probably save on expenses by finding and eliminating dead code before going to the trouble of assessing and repairing any year 2000 glitches it may contain.

✦ **Automation.** As previously discussed, there is no silver bullet software that will eliminate the year 2000 problem with a minimum of human labor. But that doesn't mean there aren't programs that can help. To whatever degree you can use software to conduct your year 2000 fix, you will probably save both time and money.

Chances are, you'll also wind up with greater accuracy. The actual work of year 2000 reprogramming is an incredibly dull affair that has been compared to resetting the time on a never-ending series of VCRs. The longer a human programmer has to spend at such tasks, the greater the likelihood of a slipup.

Accuracy is particularly crucial for the biggest part of a Y2K project—testing. Unfortunately, there are fewer software solutions for testing than for any other part of the project. This shortage has actually inspired some intrepid companies to write their own testing software. That's what UK-based NatWest (formerly National Westminster) Bank did. According to NatWest's Chief Information Technology Officer Achi Racov, hand-testing would have been "a disaster, both in terms of time, and of cost." On the other hand, creating the software from scratch was no picnic. "People told us that what we wanted to do was not possible, and they were close to being right," he says. He's not sure he would want to undertake such a project a second time.

✦ **Offshore outsourcing.** Cost savings is one big reason many companies faced with a year 2000 project are sending some of their programming work to less developed countries like India, the Philippines, and Ireland, and many countries of Eastern Europe, usually via a vendor with offices in the United States. A second benefit of this offshore outsourcing is that time-zone differences allow these programmers to work on American computers during hours when offices here are closed. They can thus avoid overtaxing and slowing down the systems. (However, this requires giving outsiders network access, which some companies may be reluctant to do.)

Cost savings can be substantial. Analysts here assume costs of more than $8,000 a month in salary and benefits for a programmer working on Y2K, while vendors in India (which is currently dominating the offshore year 2000 market) report monthly costs as low as $1,000.

Of course, the potential quality-control, communications, and cultural problems inherent in sending any work overseas exist in this case as well. But given the shortage of qualified programmers here, at least there should be fewer complaints about depriving Americans of work. "The offshore development industry has become legitimized by this problem," notes Peter de Jager. "The reality is we don't have enough people over here to do the job.

"But," he adds, "you can't outsource the responsibility for getting this done on time. If I was sending my code offshore, I'd send a manager with it, to make sure the people on the other end are working on the problem accurately and on schedule."

Reporting Year 2000 Costs

Beyond the question of how much your company must spend to fix the year 2000 problem is the question of how it records those expenses. Few aspects of the year 2000 problem are simple and straightforward, and unfortunately, accounting is not among them.

In the summer of 1996, the Emerging Issues Task Force of the Financial Accounting and Standards Board (FASB) determined that money spent to fix the year 2000 problem should be listed as an expense during the year it was spent. The only problem is that what FASB decrees governs corporate financial statements and Securities and Exchange Commission (SEC) filings. It does not have any bearing on how your company reports these expenses for tax purposes. Those questions are governed by the Internal Revenue Code, and according to those laws, year 2000 fixes most often fall into the category of capital expenditures, which must be amortized over several years. This leaves you with the worst of all possible combinations: reporting Y2K expenses in the current year on financial statements to shareholders and banks, and amortizing them for tax purposes.

A little bit of hope is offered by two provisions of the tax law. The first allows deductions for repairs that neither materially add to the value of a property nor appreciably prolong its life. Some tax professionals may argue that year 2000 fixes fit this description—and they may win the argument, depending on how the repairs are done and how they are described in vendor contracts. Historically, however, the IRS has tended to disallow same-year deductions for new types of high-cost repairs like these.

The second question is whether year 2000 repairs can be qualified as research and development costs. As such, they may also be deductible, but meeting the requirements for a deductible research expense is a complex matter, best undertaken with highly qualified tax advice.

One of the more problematic elements of this tactic is that, according to the Internal Revenue Code, research expenses must be incurred by the taxpayer, or *"upon the taxpayer's order and at his risk."* This may mean that if you use an outside vendor to work on your year 2000 problem, you cannot have a warranty that the repairs will work. If you do, the repairs are no longer at your risk, and you stand to lose your chance to deduct these costs as R&D expenses.

Think this all sounds unfair? Lawmakers may agree. Some executives, lawyers, and accountants struggling with questions of reporting year 2000 expenses are hoping that Congress will take up this issue and write new laws to clarify how year 2000 expenses are to be deducted—hopefully in the year they are incurred. Given the threat this problem poses to businesses' very survival, Congress may well decide to take the matter seriously. In any case, it's wise to involve tax-planning experts from the earliest stages of your year 2000 project.

Budgeting the Year 2000

Nearly every company that has undertaken a year 2000 repair has found itself spending more than originally planned—usually a lot more. "One of our clients came up with about $60 million to solve the problem," recalls Chuck White, a Gartner Group vice president and research director. "The more they looked at it, though, the more the budget kept going up. At this point, they're on their third pass, and the estimate is up to $140 million."

You may be tempted to think that this company is bad at making budget projections, but stories like this one are quite common. The reason is the nature of the year 2000 problem itself. As one IT executive put it: "Every time you open a door in this project, you find ten more doors behind it."

Meantime, salaries for programmers and other year 2000 expenses are growing rapidly as corporate panic sets in. The message is clear, if unpleasant: Whatever you may be planning to spend to solve the year 2000 problem, be prepared to lay out a lot more. The Gartner Group is currently predicting that the combined conversions required for year 2000 compliance and (for those dealing with Europe) the introduction of the EMU will eat up 15 to 20 percent of overall IT budgets for the next two years. That will cripple most companies' ability to undertake new technology projects.

This may be one reason IT executives have not always been quick to report the severity of the problem to top management.

The latter's response might be to pull the plug on other, more fun technology plans. Thus, not only will fixing the year 2000 project not gain your company anything except the right to stay in business, it may also preempt improvements that would have been beneficial.

You may be tempted to recoup some of this apparent waste of money by incorporating other elements (such as a general upgrade to more modern software) into your company's year 2000 project. It would certainly seem more appealing to get some sort of improved technology out of the deal if you're going to spend huge sums of money.

Don't do it. This adding of extraneous projects is what programmers call "scope creep," and it can derail your whole effort to get Y2K corrected before malfunctions start to occur. "It was a great idea five years ago," says consultant and author Ian Hayes. "Now, there just isn't time."

6

Why Lawyers Love
the Year 2000

"A few months back I read an article that said securities lawyers were salivating over the prospect of shareholder suits on year 2000 problems. Well, we get involved in securities suits, and we know a lot of securities lawyers, and I can assure you that they're not salivating. They are slobbering!"

—Steven L. Hock
Managing Partner of Operations
Thelen, Marrin, Johnson & Bridges

If the numbers in the last chapter seem imposing, keep in mind that they don't take into account one of the most expensive aspects of the year 2000 problem: the lawsuits it will inevitably inspire. In fact, it's already caused several. In one, a manufacturer sued one of its suppliers after it had to shut down its line because the factory computer automatically rejected products marked with an expiration date of "00." That case was settled out of court.

The Capers Jones report on Y2K's global impact (see Want to Know More?) predicts that legal fees for year 2000-related suits would approach $2 billion in the United States, with total damage awards perhaps reaching as high as $100 billion.

It's easy to see why the year 2000 will be a natural lawsuit producer. It's a huge problem, the stakes are very high, and everyone will be looking for someone to blame. What may be less obvious is that many of these lawsuits will not directly involve computers or computer technology at all.

Consider this possibility. You're a caterer who supplies food to functions at an elegant hotel. You sign a contract to cater an important banquet for 500 people. But on the day of the banquet, a year 2000 glitch prevents your food distributor from delivering the ingredients you need, and you are unable to provide the meals you promised. The banquet's prestigious guests wind up sending out for 200 pizzas.

Not surprisingly, the hotel sues you and, since you are in breach of contract, wins easily. Your only recourse is to turn around and sue your distributor. However, the problem did not originate with your distributor's computer, but at a warehouse three states away that should have supplied your distributor with groceries. So your distributor must now sue the warehouse.

This scenario is a good example of how a company without an in-house year 2000 glitch (or even a computer!) can still feel the impact of Y2K. And it illustrates how such a company could easily become a link in a seemingly endless chain of litigation. In fact, given the interdependent nature of today's business community, and the alacrity with which we seek legal remedies for our troubles, these domino-effect lawsuits seem a depressingly likely result of the year 2000.

Staying Out of Trouble

What are your best legal defenses against the likelihood of year 2000-related lawsuits? One obvious measure is to make sure your organization's own year 2000 problem is solved in time so that your company cannot be responsible for disrupting anyone else's business. After all, the only worse place to be than in the middle of the litigation chain is on the end where the glitch created the original problem.

Unfortunately, as noted in Chapter 1, some 80 percent of the world's businesses have started their projects too late to repair all their systems in time. If yours is among them, the next best thing, from a liability point of view, is to be able to prove that you tried your best.

This is why it's important to keep written documentation of every step in the process of your year 2000 fix. (Indeed, since many companies have found solving the year 2000 problem to be more difficult than it first seemed, you should probably keep documentation even if you currently believe all your repairs will be completed by the deadline.)

These records should demonstrate direct involvement with and commitment to fixing the year 2000 problem at the highest management levels in your organization. Steven Hock explains, "The reason it's essential is that if you end up in a courtroom, the first thing the jury is going to want to know is, what efforts did top management make to solve this problem?

"If the answer is, 'We don't have the documentation to show that,' or 'Our executive management was focusing on something else,' the jury is going to be mad and you're going to pay for it. You'll end up with executive management on the stand, and some lawyer standing there with a set of violins, saying, 'Which one of these fiddles were you playing while Rome was burning?' " The danger is real. So far, very few organizations have that top-level commitment to dealing with the year 2000 problem, and even fewer have the documentation to prove it.

When creating this documentation, you should keep in mind who its eventual readers might be. If it's rife with technical terms like "legacy system" and "windowing," or even management terms like "partnering" and "benchmarking," you may only wind up confusing the very jury you were seeking to convince.

Block That E-Mail!

Just as important as the documentation you keep is the documentation you should be careful to avoid keeping. Hock warns
about what he calls "writers of rogue memos and e-mails" who
can destroy your defense to a year 2000 lawsuit before you ever
have a year 2000 malfunction.

"Someone comes back to their workstation after a horren-
dous sixteen-hour day, working on a major conversion project
that's four weeks behind schedule," he explains. "That person
proceeds to pour out his or her heart in some memo or e-mail
that resides on a hard disk somewhere. It starts with the name
of the president of the company, and then it says: 'This guy is
out of it, he won't pay attention to our year 2000 problem. He
will not do what's necessary to get this fixed. We're screwing up
this project major league, it's going to cost our customers millions, and I'm the only one here who knows it!' Then that person
feels better, goes home and gets some sleep."

The problem is that what would otherwise amount to harm-
less venting could wind up costing you millions during a year
2000-related lawsuit. An early part of any such action is discovery, in which your opponent's lawyers have the right to examine all of your company's records and documents. Suddenly,
e-mails and other messages that their writers believed totally
private could be open to hostile view. Even e-mails that you've
deleted from your computer's hard drive can sometimes be recovered.

What can you do to prevent these damning pieces of evidence from being written? For one thing, make sure anyone in a
position to write such a document thoroughly understands the
calamity it could cause.

Another strategy is to make one of your company's lawyers
(preferably someone friendly) available and encourage your
staff to send their memos and complaints to him or her, rather
than to anyone else. That way, your employees can let off steam

whenever they have to, but their gripes will be protected by rules of attorney-client privilege and thus will not be subject to discovery.

Seek and Ye May Find

Services like the foregoing are only one reason why it's a good idea to include legal counsel in your year 2000 process from the beginning. The legal department may also be able to find some hidden sources of help in dealing with your year 2000 problem—your existing contracts with both software and hardware vendors.

In many cases, Hock says, a legal analysis of software-vendor contracts will reveal language that obligates them to participate in your year 2000 repair, or help defray its cost. (This could apply if the vendor warrants that the product will work for a given period of time, or in maintenance agreements, for example.) The analysis should include any supporting documents, such as sales brochures, that helped lead to the agreement.

If there are such obligations, the time to look for them is earlier rather than later. In cases like this, the law requires you to give the vendor adequate notice in a proper legal form. Simply writing a letter demanding the vendor's cooperation will not constitute such notice and may cost you whatever rights you had.

Your legal department should also review all future contracts with software and hardware vendors to specifically address the question of year 2000 warranties and liability. Because these will not be easy negotiations, many companies have left this issue unresolved, figuring they can deal with it at a later date. But to do so is to take a big risk for one simple reason: The year 2000 problem is now highly visible and widely recognized. And if you sign a contract that fails to address a widely known problem, you risk the presumption that your year 2000 problem is your responsibility.

There's also potential for trouble because many software-licensing situations impose limits on whether and how you can rewrite or upgrade software. Not only may working on a Y2K upgrade void any warranties by the vendors, it may actually constitute copyright infringement on your part. This could come about because the holder of a copyright (such as that for a piece of software) owns the exclusive right to create derivative work, and in past software-copyright cases, software upgrades and revisions have come to be defined as derivative works. That may mean that to upgrade or rewrite a program without the copyright owner's permission puts you in violation of federal law.

Obviously, you need to be able to upgrade your organization's software to bring it into year 2000 compliance, so it's wise to secure the copyright holder's permission to make these changes. In the event that the answer is no, a record that shows you made a good faith effort to obtain this permission may provide some legal protection.

Caution is also needed if your company is engaging in a merger or acquisition between now and the year 2000. You could find yourself saddled with someone else's year 2000 problem, and solving it might throw your own carefully orchestrated project off schedule.

A careful examination of your new acquisition's year 2000 vulnerabilities should be part of the merger's due-diligence process. Indeed, Hock says, you should approach year 2000 due diligence in the same manner as environmental due diligence, "but with even greater care because the potential liabilities are larger."

You will probably need expert help in determining just how much of a year 2000 problem the merger will entail. In the meantime, your M&A (merger and acquisition) contracts should contain year 2000 warranties, indemnifications, and possibly an escape clause in case the acquisition company's year 2000 problem proves unmanageable.

Shareholder Suits

Publicly held companies whose business suffers because of the year 2000 problem, or which are forced to pay large sums to head it off, are almost certain to find themselves facing shareholder lawsuits. In these cases, officers and directors of the company can be held personally liable for damages.

Potential liability arises out of management's obligation to provide a Management Discussion and Analysis of Operations and Trends (MD&A) as part of its 10K financial filings with the SEC. The MD&A should address all trends and conditions that could have a material effect on future financial results—a description that squarely fits the year 2000 problem.

Some lawyers are predicting that boilerplate disclaimers, stating that the year 2000 problem might negatively impact performance, will begin to be included in most MD&As. In 1996, that hadn't happened yet. The only mention of the year 2000 problem Hock could find in a 10K report was from a small insurance company that claimed it had a business advantage, having already solved the problem. He's betting the year 2000 problem will be mentioned more often in 1997 and 1998 filings.

Underwriting Y2K

When it comes to the question of insurance for the year 2000 problem, there's good news and bad news. The good news is that the same lawyers who carefully review your contracts with information technology providers should also take a look at your existing insurance contracts. Though they were probably not written with the year 2000 in mind, it's just possible that these contracts provide some year 2000 coverage.

The idea is that altering computer data to accommodate needed changes to the system might constitute property damage, which is covered under many policies. It may be especially helpful if the policy covers "valuable business records." The idea that all or part of a year 2000 fix may be covered as property damage is nothing more than a legal theory at this point. But given the expense involved in most year 2000 fixes, it's certain that, sooner or later, some enterprising lawyer will put this theory to the test.

That, such as it is, is the good news. The bad news is that whatever coverage you can scrounge through creative interpretation of current and past insurance contracts may well be the only year 2000 insurance you ever have. As the problem grows in prominence, more and more insurance companies are adding riders to their contracts that specifically exclude Y2K. In the meantime, although some companies are venturing cautiously into this market, so far it's extremely difficult to buy insurance specifically aimed at the year 2000 problem. And even if you can buy it, it's likely to be an expensive proposition.

American International Group (AIG) is one of a very, very few insurers specifically offering year 2000 coverage—of a sort. The sort is called "blended" or "finite" insurance, and it works like this. Depending on your company's perceived Y2K risk, AIG will charge you 60 to 80 percent of the coverage bought. This means that if you want $100 million in insurance, the policy's premium will be between $60 and $80 million. However, at the end of the coverage period (say, 2002), AIG will rebate 90 percent of the premium paid, minus whatever losses were actually incurred.

"Through a premium mechanism, I'm taking the client on as reinsurer to share the risk with me," explains AIG Executive Vice President Robert Omahne. The reason is simple, he says. Insurance is based on the idea that calamities have predictable costs, that you can look at a "historical pool" of events (such as a building burning down) and make an educated guess how much such an event will typically cost to rectify.

Not so with the year 2000. The changeover of a millennium (at least during the computer age) is completely unprecedented. With no past events to compare it with, calculations as to Y2K's eventual cost are uncertain at best. And, Omahne says, "when you price on uncertainty, the price becomes very expensive."

If you think you can't afford it, don't worry. You probably won't get the chance to buy the insurance in any case. AIG is carefully screening companies that apply to make sure they have their year 2000 repair well in hand—along with some carefully thought-out contingency plans. Those that pass AIG's initial review get an on-site examination by an outside year 2000 consultant before AIG offers them a policy. If they do not pass muster, Omahne says, AIG will not offer them insurance at all—or only on a dollar-for-dollar basis (i.e., $100 of insurance costs $100). So far, he adds, the company has turned down the majority of the companies that applied.

"Our appetite for this business is not huge," he explains. "If we write fifty of these, that's about all we want to write." Though AIG specializes in unusual and difficult insurance situations, he says, "we're doing it in a very cautious way. Because we know we could lose big on this."

7

The People Problem

"In 1997–1998, most of IS [the information systems in-dustry] will wake up and realize they need to increase staff by 30 percent, or some such number, over two years to complete the year 2000 project. If we all require even a 10 percent to 15 percent increase in skilled staff, supply cannot meet demand."

—John Burns
Canadian Imperial Bank of Commerce

As we have seen, the year 2000 is more of a business problem than a technology problem. So it makes sense that the single biggest obstacle to a successful Y2K conversion project is not hardware, or even software, but finding—and keeping—the right people to do the job. Y2K is, among other things, a human resources challenge of major proportions.

To begin with, the American IT industry as a whole is facing a struggle when it comes to staffing. In February 1997, the Information Technology Association of America (ITAA) released a study that showed there were 190,000 unfilled technology jobs at medium-size and large American corporations. ITAA reported that the shortage of skilled technology workers would hamper the growth of American companies and force them to send technology work offshore (as is already happening with billions of dollars worth of year 2000 code conversion).

ITAA called for legislation to examine the problem and create a national skills training program to help close the technology worker gap, and Senator John Warner (R-Va.) has established a commission to do just that. Similar programs have already proved effective in a number of other countries.

If the growing shortage of skilled information technology workers is a general problem throughout corporate America, it takes on crisis proportions when it comes to the year 2000. The biggest reason for the crisis is COBOL. COBOL is a computer language, written specifically for business applications and used on mainframe computers, that was most popular in the 1970s and 1980s. As noted earlier, there are more lines of code in COBOL than in any other language residing in the world's computers.

Obviously, not all year 2000 conversion jobs will need to be done in COBOL. But this language makes up such a big piece of the pie that Y2K software developers and consultants routinely focus on it to the exclusion of all others.

Unfortunately, COBOL is now obsolete, rendered so by the growing ascendance of client/server (rather than mainframe) technology, LANs, and programming in languages like UNIX and Java. Most college computer science programs haven't taught COBOL for years. What this adds up to is a huge demand for COBOL programmers to work on the year 2000 problem, a limited supply available to do the job, and no prospect of new ones among the crop of graduating college seniors.

There's a new T-shirt rumored to be in circulation: "COBOL programmers are back, and we're mad!" The joke is based on fact; computing conferences abound with stories of retired COBOL programmers lured off the golf course with promises of six-figure salaries.

The situation is so desperate that there are technology companies offering crash courses in COBOL to those hankering to get rich quick on the year 2000 problem. For that's who's likeliest to study this language. Serious programmers might think twice because once the year 2000 has passed, it will doubtless sink back into obscurity. (I should add that COBOL is only the most widely used of several languages that are obsolete but needed for the year 2000 fix. FORTRAN is another example of the same phenomenon, though on a smaller scale.)

"I don't know if you're having trouble hiring people, but I am," John Bruns, manager of administrative systems at McCormick & Company, Inc., told an audience of IT managers recently. He went on to describe his encounter with a twenty-six-year-old COBOL programmer who refused to work for less than $120,000 a year. Outraged, Bruns sent her on her way. "I just didn't think a twenty-six-year-old, with only six years' work experience, had the stature to command that kind of salary," he says. "But somebody will pay it."

The Gartner Group has estimated that year 2000 repair costs will go up by 20 to 25 percent a year from now until the year 2000, and rising compensation for programmers is the reason for the expected increase. It's hard to predict how high these bidding wars might go.

But worse than driving up the cost of your year 2000 repair, the programmer crunch could derail it altogether if key personnel are tempted away to other jobs. In fact, according to Peter de Jager, smart managers should work on the assumption that this will happen. He believes you should plan a 10 percent turnover every month among your year 2000 staff.

Besides writing a blank check for COBOL programmers and project managers, what can your company do to help attract people with the right expertise, and more important, keep the ones you already have?

A Human Resources Strategy

You'll be best equipped to deal with this problem if you go into your year 2000 project with the understanding that hiring qualified people will be difficult, and that your organization will see some defections.

From this perspective, it's clear that your human resources executives should be heavily involved in your year 2000 project as early in the process as possible. Your best defense against the year 2000 talent shortage is to create a carefully planned and delineated HR strategy that specifically addresses this challenge, at both the programmer level and the management level.

This strategy should consider how to motivate and retain both programmers and other information technology staff, as well as project managers and other executives involved in overseeing, coordinating, controlling, and tracking the project. Here are some options to consider.

1. **Cash rewards for year 2000 performance.** Many companies are wisely hesitant to give lavish raises to IT professionals involved in the year 2000 project because doing so will create an awkward situation later, after the project is done. On the other hand, as Bruns noted, if you don't come across with big bucks, chances are someone else will.

What can you do? One solution is to offer money in the form of one-time bonuses or incentives. The information services area as a whole has been slow to adopt the sort of performance incentives that other disciplines (most obviously sales) have long used to boost their personnel's performance. But that's a situation that should change, and the year 2000 project is an excellent place to start.

In "Compensation and Year 2000," an article in the *Year/ 2000 Journal* (see Want to Know More?), Dave Bettinger (senior communications specialist for L.L. Bean) proposes an individualized set of incentives for everyone working on the year 2000 fix. In addition to their regular salary and benefits, employees should be offered rewards at specific milestones during the life of the project, as well as a significant bonus if they stay on until the work is completed.

In Bettinger's model, a prototypical programmer earning

$40,000 a year (but able to substantially increase that salary by leaving for another company) would be offered a $10,000 bonus for signing on to the year 2000 project. For every project milestone that she delivered a month or more ahead of schedule, she would receive another $10,000. She'd get $5,000 if the milestone was on time, and no bonus if it was late. Once the entire project was completed, she would receive $20,000 for finishing on time, $15,000 if it was less than a month late, $10,000 if it was less than two months late, and no bonus if it was later than that.

It may sound like a lot of bother, not to mention expense, but it will certainly be both more expensive and more bothersome to hire someone new and bring that person up to speed if members of your Y2K staff leave for other jobs. This is why many of the companies that are taking a strong approach to the year 2000 have included some form of reward system in their plans, though the numbers may differ significantly from Bettinger's.

2. **Rewards for non-year 2000 staffers.** Putting a lucrative reward system in place for your year 2000 staff can be a double-edged sword. You might gain greater loyalty and enthusiasm from those who are working on the project, but alienate their colleagues at work on ongoing software maintenance—also something your organization shouldn't be without. This is why Bettinger recommends using Y2K as an impetus to bring rewards-based compensation to your whole IT operation.

3. **Noncash rewards.** It's often repeated, but true: Noncash rewards can be very powerful motivators, especially if used in conjunction with cash rewards. These could be as simple as plaques, gift certificates, or special mugs for completing portions of a year 2000 project. More meaningful rewards might include increased responsibility, outings, or the opportunity to work more flexible hours.

Whatever motivators you choose to use, this is the time to pay some close attention to team building among your technology workers, especially if you have not done so in the past.

4. **Training opportunities.** Programmers—especially those working in ancient languages like COBOL—may well be wondering what will become of them after the year 2000. This is a very good question.

The computer industry is changing so rapidly that it's a challenge for anyone, whatever his or her responsibilities, to stay up-to-date. A programmer working on a year 2000 project may have to spend workdays, evenings, and weekends trying to fix an antiquated system before the deadline. He will have little hope of keeping up with changing technology at the same time.

Assuming these are people with a career commitment to computing, and not retirees adding to their nest egg or (as in some anecdotes) Ivy League graduates who've found a quick way to pay off their student loans, your programming staff will likely be very much behind the times when this project is over. With this in mind, you can see how the promise of time off for training could be a powerful incentive for technology professionals at work on the year 2000 project. It would also show them that your company is committed to them for more than just the next couple of years.

The situation is a little different for year 2000 project managers. In their case, the outdated technology will be less of a handicap, while the expertise they gain by working on this complex and difficult project will stand them in good stead throughout their careers. But here too, you may want to increase their loyalty, as well as their value to your organization, by supplementing the experience with formal project management training.

5. **Overstaffing.** One of the few things less appealing than the thought of hiring a COBOL programmer at $120,000 a year is the thought of hiring two of them. But if your organization is dependent on its computing power, you should probably consider doing just that. Even if de Jager's prediction of 10 percent a month proves to be too pessimistic, your department will almost certainly suffer from some attrition. Having more staff than you

strictly need can help ensure that all the work will be done in time. And since year 2000 projects routinely turn out to be many times more complex than they at first appear, there's an excellent chance that there'll be plenty of work to go around.

An interesting variant, especially for those on the management side of the project, is to keep some non-year 2000 staff members peripherally involved so that they can step in if there's a sudden vacancy. "One of the things we're doing is to bring additional individuals into our Year 2000 program offices to work on the project," says Irene Dec, vice president of corporate information technology and companywide Year 2000 project manager for Prudential Insurance Co. of America. "They sit in on meetings, and spend about 20 to 25 percent of their time working on the year 2000," she notes. "That will make for an easy transition, should it become necessary."

Franklin D. Roosevelt once said, in reference to the Great Depression, "Above all, try something." The sentiment applies here as well. Whatever strategy you adopt to deal with the shortage of information technology professionals, your worst choice is to do nothing, in the hope that business will continue as usual.

As this briefing goes to press, concern about Y2K is building fast in the media and throughout corporate America. Companies that have done little or nothing about this problem (which, according to some estimates, may be most of them) are waking up in a panic to the realization that the year 2000 can mean real trouble for their organizations and that the time to do something about it is running out fast.

That panic will create a feeding frenzy, with increasingly desperate companies willing to pay almost anything for help with what they have finally realized is a business survival issue. If you are not prepared, you will almost certainly lose key IT personnel during your own year 2000 project—when you can least afford it.

8

Getting Outside Help

"Everyone who can print up a business card that says 'Year 2000 Consulting' has done so. Some of them know what they're doing. Some of them don't."

—Ian Hayes
Principal, Clarity Consulting Co-Author
The Year 2000 Software Crisis:
Challenge of the Century

With the year 2000 deadline drawing nearer, and the prospects of hiring extra IT staff looking grim, executives faced with Y2K are doing the logical thing: turning to outside consultants for help with their year 2000 projects.

The consultants are out there. Hundreds of new Y2K consulting firms have started up since the problem first came to prominence in late 1994. Many of these are software development firms or consultants who've now made the year 2000 their special focus. And the management consulting arms of the "Big Six" accounting firms are giving the year 2000 serious attention.

Most companies of any size at all are working with at least one vendor, and often three or more. It's easy to see why. An outside vendor can bring a variety of advantages to the project.

✦ **Flexible staffing.** As discussed in the last chapter, it may be difficult for you to hire all the programmers you need to solve the year 2000 problem. But if you do manage, you'll have another problem after the repair is completed and you no longer need quite so many of them. Although some additional staff to deal with Y2K may still be necessary, working with a vendor can keep the numbers under control.

✦ **Availability of IT staff for other projects.** Conversely, whether you add staff or not, your in-house IT professionals will find their work schedules dominated by Y2K for the two or more years the project lasts. Given the speed of technological advances today, two years is way too long to be "out of the loop." You may get your year 2000 repairs completed, but your company will have become technologically out-of-date in the process.

✦ **More efficient tools.** IT people talk about finding "best of breed" tools (i.e., software) to attack the year 2000 problem. For though there is no silver bullet, there are programs that can help, at least to some degree, at every stage of work. A vendor who has already been through the year 2000 repair process at other companies has probably experimented with a number of these tools, and knows which ones work best.

✦ **Methodology.** Since vendors have probably experimented with different tools, they should also have worked out a method of attack for the year 2000. Remember that one of the hard parts of this job is figuring out which of several interconnected systems should be fixed first. A vendor who can answer questions like this is a valuable asset indeed.

✦ **Cost.** Working with a vendor will usually provide savings over going it alone. And the difference can be significant. Irene Dec reports that the estimate for fixing Prudential's year 2000 problem internally was $150 million—without considering lost opportunity costs for the company's IT staff. By working with an outside vendor (and by moving to address the problem earlier rather than later), they were able to reduce that estimate to between $100 and $110 million.

✦ **Offshore work.** Vendors can save you money in many ways, but one of the biggest is by arranging to have some of your Y2K work done in places like India, Eastern Europe, Ireland, or the Philippines where salaries are lower and more programmers are available for the job. This practice is so common that most American year 2000 vendors work with offshore software-conversion facilities in these or other developing countries, and there are many offshore vendors with offices here as well. (Some pros and cons of offshore outsourcing are discussed in Chapter 5.) Needless to say, sending your work to a developing country is something you'll need a vendor's help to do.

Buying in a Seller's Market

While hiring a vendor to help with your company's year 2000 problem is clearly a good idea, finding one who is both willing and able to do the job may be more difficult than you expect. Mounting panic over the year 2000 has driven a growing demand for these services. Meanwhile, the obstacles to hiring and retention described in the last chapter are having their effect on vendors as well.

At the end of 1996, the Gartner Group was predicting that, by mid-1997, year 2000 vendors would no longer be accepting new clients, and any company that had not already contracted whatever help it needed would be left out in the cold.

As this briefing goes to press (in the summer of 1997), that has not yet happened. O'Connell says it still will, perhaps around the end of 1997. In the meantime, it certainly is a seller's market out there.

Faced with these narrowing prospects, how should you go about choosing a year 2000 consultant? Very, very quickly. Because of the danger of getting no outside help, or getting lower-quality help than you need, this is not a question you can afford to study for long. "If I didn't have a vendor at this point, I'd hurry up and pick one," Dec says.

The usual first step in selecting a contractor for a major project is to issue a request for proposals (RFP), but—unless RFPs are legally mandated for your company—you should consider skipping this step. For one thing, you don't have time. With just over two years to go until New Year's Eve 1999, your company may have just enough time to get its mission-critical systems fixed. This might no longer be true, however, by the time you've drafted an RFP, sent it out, evaluated the responses, and made your final selection.

And even if you do have time to go through this whole process, chances are your prospective consultants won't. They're in an industry where demand is greater than supply. Presumably, they're hard at work trying their best to accomplish a deeply complex project, with a very short deadline, for the clients they already have. If they're willing to respond to a detailed RFP, you might ask yourself why they have so much time on their hands.

Another common method for choosing a software development firm is to send the same sample project to several candidates. This may be a good way of making a comparison, but once again, it will take time you can't afford to lose. Instead, Ian Hayes and Bill Ulrich suggest something more useful: sending a different project to each prospective vendor, with clear specifications (so that each will be compatible with your post-Y2K systems). This allows you to make some progress on your year 2000 project while evaluating prospective vendors.

What to Look For

Assuming you still have some options when you seek out a year 2000 consultant, what qualities should you look for?

1. **History with your firm.** Since the year 2000 is a business survival issue, you should have absolute trust in the people you hire to help you work on it. This is one reason why Prudential

made a prior relationship one of its criteria for selecting year 2000 vendors.

Another good reason for doing this is the prospect that your two companies will continue to work together on other projects in the future. "Some consultants have said, 'I'm going to make a lot of money over the next couple of years, then I'm going to take off,'" Hayes reports. "Great! They'll be leaving just when these things are getting implemented."

The year 2000 problem is not going to end when the year 2000 arrives. Companies that rushed to get their most vital systems fixed will still have less crucial repairs waiting to be made. And at least some of the newly repaired systems will turn out to have bugs or other problems that the repair itself created. These are all good reasons why you need your vendor relationship to continue past December 31, 1999.

2. **Reputation.** If you can't, or don't want to, use a vendor you've worked with before, the next best thing is to find a company with a solid standing in the industry. Managers working on Y2K are usually quite willing, and even eager, to share information, so gathering this information about prospective vendor firms should not be difficult.

The Big Six accounting firms (which some now call the Big Six consulting firms) offer reputation and a high degree of stability. The drawback, of course, is that competition to hire these companies will be fierce.

It is also a plus if the firm in question has received the Information Technology Association of America's certification for its year 2000 methodology. Firms that have gained certification have had their methods carefully audited by ITAA professionals.

Besides the company's reputation, the reputation of the individual manager or managers who'll be responsible for your year 2000 project is of great importance. Don't forget to check this out as well, as part of your evaluation process.

3. **Good subcontractor relationships.** Year 2000 projects are almost always more complicated than they at first appear, yet

the deadline for getting them done can't be moved. Given that combination, it's highly possible that a well-meaning vendor might find itself with more work than it can handle. You should know up front whether your consultant has good relationships with subcontractors in case the former winds up needing extra help to complete your project.

4. **Methodology.** According to Hayes, the vendor you choose should have a well-thought-out, written methodology for managing a year 2000 project. "If they won't show it to you and let you look through it, then they don't have a methodology," he says.

Likewise, he notes, you should ask vendors which year 2000 software tools they work with. If they have some experience in the field, they should have formed some definite opinions about which software works most efficiently. Be wary of vendors who say they can work with "whatever you've got."

You're Still Responsible

There are a wide range of formulas for working with year 2000 consultants. At one end of the scale, they might simply provide extra programming staff to work in your IT department, or supply training and information to "jump-start" your year 2000 project and help you get going quickly. Or, you may ask a contractor to completely take over one or more of your year 2000 subprojects, or oversee the entire project for your whole organization.

Even if you choose this last option, however, the ultimate responsibility rests with your company, and you still need people at your end to track and manage both the vendor relationship and the repairs themselves. This is why, no matter how much outsourcing you do, if you want your year 2000 project to succeed, your company will still need its own project management team.

Not long ago, I overheard an IT executive ask a consultant from a Big Six firm whether it was true that his company was no longer taking on new year 2000 clients. No, he answered, that rumor wasn't quite true . . . but he did allow that the company was pretty much dictating the terms of its contracts. And, he said, it wasn't signing any that gave guarantees for year 2000 repairs.

As discussed in Chapter 5, there may be tax reasons why you wouldn't want to sign such a contract, either. But even if you did, and even if you found a vendor who agreed, the ultimate responsibility for your firm's year 2000 problem would remain yours. After all, having good grounds for a lawsuit will be small consolation if your firm is forced to close its doors because a mission-critical system failed.

9

Your Year 2000 Team

Who should be responsible for overseeing your organization's year 2000 project? If you've read the preceding chapters, you know by now that this is something your information technology staff may not be able to handle on its own. In fact, the year 2000 problem is a major project-management challenge. Who owns the project, and how it is driven within your organization, will determine more than anything else whether critical systems will be repaired in time. This question is more important than what software you use or what computer systems you have. I would argue that it's even more important than which outside consultants you get to help you with the project.

Your company's year 2000 effort needs these three things:

1. Absolute commitment (not just lip service and money) from top-level management
2. Highly capable, skilled, motivated people to drive the project within the organization
3. High-level sponsorship and a high profile (so that everyone within the organization working with any computer or computerized device gives this project the needed priority)

Without these three elements, it will probably be difficult to get mission-critical repairs accomplished in time.

One Central Office

If yours is a large or midsize organization with separate departments, divisions, or other business areas, the first question you'll
have to answer is whether to structure your Y2K effort as a separate project within each of your company's areas ("enterprises,"
as IT people call them) or to have one central office coordinate
Y2K for your whole organization from top to bottom. As it turns
out, this is not one of those issues where different solutions are
more effective for different organizations. No matter who you
are or what your organization does (or even whether it's divided
into otherwise autonomous businesses or divisions), your year
2000 effort will work better if it is centrally coordinated.

To begin with, there are all the usual advantages of a cen-
tralized effort, such as economies of scale and greater negotiat-
ing leverage. More to the point, by having a central office that
coordinates all year 2000 work, you can save duplication of effort
from one division to another. Given that time to solve this problem is rapidly running out, you cannot afford to duplicate learn-
ing experiences and experimentation with software tools from
one division to another.

But even more important than that, consider that the year
2000 project is a mammoth job of coordination. Today's computers are deeply interdependent, routinely working with both software and data imported from other computers, either on disk
or (more commonly) over a network. Every computer in your
company is probably interacting with many other computers
within your company. And, because today's businesses are as
interdependent as today's computers, it is probably exchanging
data with computers outside your company as well.

Because of all these connections, the only way to handle
a year 2000 conversion is with a complex network of both
"bridges" (intermediary programs that help noncompliant and
compliant systems understand each other, and which must be
"burned" once the systems at both ends are compliant) and

"firewalls" (barriers that prevent contaminating data, such as viruses, and non-year 2000 compliant data from entering the system).

When one central office has companywide jurisdiction over all the year 2000 conversions, that office can keep a master plan for choreographing all these changes and interfaces. It can establish organizationwide standards for how the changes will be carried out and what types of solutions will be used (for remember that, from a programming point of view, there are many different ways to deal with Y2K). It can establish and enforce guidelines about which systems are mission-critical and need to be fixed first. And it will give you the best possible chance of having those systems fixed in time.

The Best Managers—Not the Best Techies

Who should be on your year 2000 team? The word from companies that have battled this problem is that the people involved are more important than the technology. Obviously, good technology is a cornerstone of any successful year 2000 project. But when staffing the team that will oversee and coordinate this effort, the best strategy is to choose those whose skills make them effective leaders, managers, organizers, and project managers rather than those who have the greatest technical knowledge.

Special care should be taken when selecting the person who will head up the project. It's clear, of course, that he or she should be someone with all the skills mentioned above. What may be less clear, until you think about it, is that he or she also needs to be a director of your organization, someone at the vice president level or higher. At first glance, this might seem like managerial overkill, but there are many good arguments for making the head of your year 2000 team a high-level executive. Among them are the following.

◆ **Existing lines of communication.** This person will need to report on the progress of the year 2000 project to your board of directors or top executives. (After all, these are the folks who may be personally liable if a year 2000-related business reversal prompts a shareholder lawsuit.)

It will make life a lot simpler if she or he is already reporting at (or near) this level in the natural order of things. It will help this issue get the serious attention it deserves from these top executives—something that hasn't always happened at many companies. It may also be easier for an executive at this level to tell your directors the unvarnished truth about how bad the problem is and how quickly and successfully repairs are being accomplished—something else that hasn't always happened in the past.

✦ **Resources.** Having a VP at the head of your year 2000 effort will also send a message to the rest of your organization about the seriousness and high priority of this issue. It will mean the effort is accorded both the resources and the internal cooperation it requires. Remember that computer users throughout your company will be asked to stop what they are doing and temporarily relinquish their desktops and terminals, answer questionnaires and surveys about what programs they have and use, and generally inconvenience themselves while the year 2000 problem is being resolved. It will help to have a high-level executive doing the asking.

✦ **External communications.** It's my belief that people who are dealing with the year 2000 problem will increasingly find themselves in the spotlight as the year 2000 approaches. Certainly, the first time a company in your industry has a newsworthy year 2000 mishap, the local and trade press are likely to call. So may some of your customers, business partners, and investors.

Before all this happens, you should ask yourself who you want to be the public face of your organization on the subject of the year 2000 problem. It should be someone who can represent your company at year 2000 user groups and conferences, and someone who can both answer tough questions and know what not to say—someone who'll command the respect of both your customers and the press.

What's more, you may recall from Chapter 6 that if you ever find yourself on the defending side of a year 2000-related lawsuit, it will be important to prove that this issue had the attention and commitment of your top management. The fact that a high-level executive headed up the effort can help.

The Rest of the Team

Who else should be on your year 2000 project team? Here are some of the functions and people who should be represented or covered.

+ **Information technology.** Even if all or most of your re-programming effort is being outsourced, you need your own technology people to be involved in the project.

+ **Human resources.** You will need an HR strategy to deal with the hiring and retention problems the year 2000 is bound to cause. Involve these executives in the process early rather than late to stop attrition before it happens.

+ **Legal.** This department's members also should be involved early in the process. They can help review vendor agreements and other legal documents to cut down on your future Y2K liability. They can help you structure the project itself to make you less vulnerable to liability suits. And by carefully reviewing existing contracts, they may be able to generate some "found money" to help defray the cost of the fix.

+ **Financial.** Because of the expense involved, it's a good idea to keep financial people abreast of all the changes and cost estimates as they happen. They can also help structure Y2K cost reporting for maximum tax advantages.

+ **Internal audit.** Helping with a year 2000 project falls naturally into this department's range of activities.

✦ **Risk assessment.** This is also a department that will naturally concern itself with the year 2000 problem.

✦ **Individual enterprises within your company.** If your company is divided into autonomous divisions, then each one should have a representative on your year 2000 team.

Of course, depending on your company's size, some of these may not apply. But, for the same reason that it's important to coordinate your company's entire year 2000 project from one central office, it's important to get every department that is directly involved with the issue involved in your effort as well.

The Five Phases of Y2K

Although year 2000 projects differ from company to company, there are many aspects of every Y2K fix that remain the same, whether you do the work yourself or hire an outside consultant to take over most of it for you. Though the timing may vary, every year 2000 project must go through the same five phases:

1. Assessment
2. Planning
3. Implementation
4. Testing
5. Deployment

How you approach each phase and how long it takes can vary widely, depending on how your company is managing its year 2000 tasks. But here are some constants to keep in mind at each phase.

✦ **Assessment.** A few months ago, I listened as a representative from a software vendor explained how her company could help clients through their year 2000 fixes. "First, you do your assessment," she began, and then detailed what her company would do at that phase. "Once you're done with your assessment, you're ready to move on to the next step," she continued.

There's only one problem with this. The woman was giving the presentation in the spring of 1997—close to the time some experts claim is the cutoff point for beginning a successful year 2000 project. I don't mean to criticize either the company or the salesperson, but there's a serious question as to whether any organization should, today, take the time to finish the assessment part of its project before starting on the fix itself. Indeed, most year 2000 experts who once recommended a thorough and complete inventory of affected programs now speak against a long assessment phase—because it could seriously jeopardize the success of the whole project.

✦ **Planning.** Instead of a lengthy assessment of what programs you have, and what the impact of two-digit years might be, it's a better idea to do triage. Identify exactly which systems are most critical to your organization's welfare, and plan a strategy that will allow time to deal with those. This will mean making some painful decisions, but it is a process nearly every company that deals with its year 2000 problem will have to go through.

At this stage, your year 2000 team will make decisions about exactly what form repairs will take, as well as settling such basic questions as whether to expand year fields to four digits or use a "window" or "procedural" approach. (See Chapter 5 for a more detailed discussion of these choices.) This is also when the team should establish a master plan so the members know which systems are being fixed in what order. Because most systems today are connected to several others, and "bridges" must be inserted between them to keep compliant and noncompliant systems working together, the planning phase has to be a masterpiece of choreography.

Remember that assessment and planning together make up less than 20 percent of the effort involved in a typical year 2000 project.

✦ **Implementation.** This is the actual work of year 2000 conversion. Of all the stages of a year 2000 fix, this is probably the one where software "tools" can help the most. Though far from easy, this is the most straightforward part of a year 2000 project. It should make up 15 percent of the effort or less.

✦ **Testing.** Once a program has been rewritten to accept dates in the next century without malfunctioning, it must be tested—both to make sure the solution worked and to see if alterations to the program accidentally created or revealed some other bug. This requires taking the program offline and fooling the host computer into the belief that the current year is 2000 or later.

As I mentioned in Chapter 2, this testing process is the biggest, most difficult, and most time-consuming phase of any year 2000 project. It may account for 60 percent of the effort or more. There are now some software tools on the market to help with testing (most of them recently released), but I believe that for most organizations, in most situations, testing will still be largely a manual affair. For this reason, it is usually the part of the project that can most fruitfully be sent to an offshore vendor in a country where labor is more plentiful and less expensive.

✦ **Deployment.** Once a system has been rendered year 2000-compliant, it's ready to be deployed within your company as the last step in your year 2000 project. Despite diligent testing efforts, users may still discover a variety of glitches that the year 2000 upgrade left behind. Be prepared for this. It's one reason why wise managers set themselves a completion date of December 1998. That will give the newly converted software some time to be tested in the real world.

10

Strategic Decisions: How Prudential Is Handling Y2K

So far, I've given you general instructions on how to manage a year 2000 project. Now, let's look at how one specific company has structured its own effort. When discussing Y2K at Prudential Insurance Co. of America, I should begin by stressing that the year 2000 project there is not a typical Y2K fix. The effort was begun in the summer of 1995, with the full understanding by the company's CEO that the year 2000 could create a potential crisis.

Although Y2K can cripple any company in any industry, both insurance companies and financial service companies are particularly vulnerable because they depend heavily on computerization, and because their businesses deal with long periods of time (often reaching into the future as well as the past).

Prudential's four main lines of business are health care, life insurance, investments, and securities. So the company was threatened on several fronts and was determined to deal with those threats in time. "We will not let this touch our customers. We're really committed to that," explains Irene Dec, vice president of corporate information technology and Prudential's Year 2000 program director.

As Prudential examined its year 2000 risks and options, it established a set of eight operating principles to guide it through the year 2000 project. They are:

1. Applications will be repaired or replaced based on rigorous risk and cost analyses.
2. Replacement and contingency plans must be in place by December 31, 1996.
3. Redundant applications performing similar functions will be consolidated where appropriate.
4. Parallel development activities will be carefully researched and assessed to ensure against jeopardizing the timely success of year 2000 maintenance. (In other words, the company would be wary of "scope creep"— the tendency to undertake other improvements at the same time as a year 2000 repair.)
5. All new software will be certified (as year 2000-compliant) before purchase and installation.
6. Standard date formats will be employed in new development. (In Prudential's case, that standard is four-digit years.)
7. All applications require Prudential's in-house year 2000 compliance certification.
8. All infrastructures (hardware, operating systems, etc.) require compliance certification.

Although Prudential has seven separate business units, its entire year 2000 effort is overseen by Dec, who reports directly to the company's CIO. Dec's office is staffed with ten Prudential employees and eight staffers from external year 2000 consultants. One of the office's functions is to assist the business units in meeting their own year 2000 objectives through a company-wide liaison program. This way, the central office learns right away if some part of the year 2000 project is falling behind and can implement a SWAT team approach by sending troubleshoot-ers to help get repairs back on schedule. (See exhibit.)

It's a huge job. Prudential has more than 800 computer ap-plications and some 100,000 programs in its software portfolio. Its computers run about 110 million lines of code, and current estimates for repair costs are about $110 million.

Further, about 10 percent of the company's software portfo-lio is in "distributed" systems—that is, in client/server systems and in people's desktop computers. Dec's office is overseeing these repairs as well, and so her staff is engaged in a massive communication effort to make sure PC users throughout the company are aware of the year 2000 problem. This means mak-ing sure each user cooperates in having his or her system checked out; being careful that the data users import on disk or download through a network is not truncating the year to two digits; and also upgrading whatever desktop applications (such

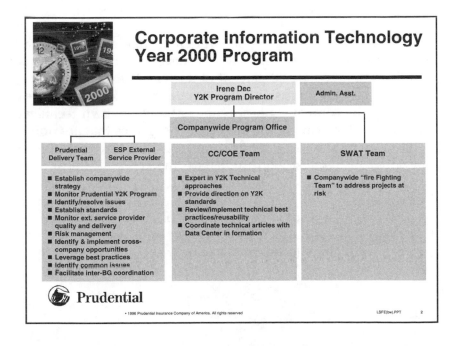

Corporate Information Technology Year 2000 Program

	Irene Dec Y2K Program Director	Admin. Asst.
	Companywide Program Office	

Prudential Delivery Team	ESP External Service Provider	CC/COE Team	SWAT Team
■ Establish companywide strategy ■ Monitor Prudential Y2K Program ■ Identify/resolve issues ■ Establish standards ■ Monitor ext. service provider quality and delivery ■ Risk management ■ Identify & implement cross-company opportunities ■ Leverage best practices ■ Identify common issues ■ Facilitate inter-BG coordination		■ Expert in Y2K Technical approaches ■ Provide direction on Y2K standards ■ Review/implement technical best practices/reusability ■ Coordinate technical articles with Data Center in formation	■ Companywide "fire Fighting Team" to address projects at risk

Prudential

LSFE(bw).PPT   2

as word processor or spreadsheet programs) aren't year 2000-compliant.

For tracking purposes, Dec has divided Prudential's year 2000 project into three basic areas:

+ **Applications.** This covers the company's entire portfolio of computer programs. A strategic review will determine whether each application should be repaired, replaced, or retired as part of the year 2000 project.
+ **Infrastructure.** This covers hardware (the mainframes and personal computers) as well as telecommunications facilities, building complexes owned by Prudential (many of which have functions such as elevators and heat controlled by computers), and the corporate airplane fleet.
+ **External partnerships.** This covers all the company's relationships with outside parties, including suppliers, government agencies, and business partners.

Another strategic decision Prudential made at the beginning of its year 2000 project was to have external consultants handle approximately 80 percent of its year 2000 programming work. Though this decision saved Prudential money, it was inspired by the company's desire not to tie up its own technical staff during the years of the project. "Companies that are doing a purely internal fix are making some decisions as to their future development, because you can't have the same technical staff working on new technology and fixing the year 2000 problem," Dec explains.

"We did not want to dedicate a lot of our own resources to this project. We are a technology leader now, and we want to still be a technology leader in the year 2000."

11

Partnering Y2K

Making sure all your company's mission-critical systems are year 2000-compliant is a huge job. But even so, it may not be enough to keep you out of trouble with the year 2000. You could still have a business reversal or even failure if a supplier or "partner" company you rely on for materials or services can't meet its obligations because of its own Y2K-related snafu.

What can you do about it? As always with the year 2000, your worst choice is to do nothing.

1. **Make a careful assessment.** Begin by assessing year 2000 readiness at those suppliers whose products you depend on for your business. If you're working with a year 2000 consulting firm, it may offer such supplier assessments as part of its service and may be better equipped to judge other companies' compliance and identify potential problems.

What if you do find a problem? Your response depends on your relationship with your supplier firm. If you're in a "partnering" relationship, it might be appropriate for your company to help with the supplier's year 2000 fix. In other situations, that might not make sense.

2. **Let them know you mean business.** Whatever else you do, it's essential to let the supplier know that year 2000 compliance is vital to your continued relationship. Here again, a good

year 2000 consultant can help, playing "bad cop" by telling the supplier that things must improve or the consultant will recommend a switch.

3. **Explore alternatives.** Switching is something you should be prepared to do in any case. Unless you are thoroughly confident of your supplier's year 2000 readiness, it's in your best interest to line up backup vendors that can step into the void if your regular supplier can't deliver. These backup suppliers should also be evaluated for year 2000 compliance so you can count on them to be able to meet your needs.

4. **Be especially careful of just-in-time.** Does your company work on just-in-time inventory? If so, you will be very vulnerable if one of your suppliers is prevented from delivering product on time (or at all) because of a year 2000 glitch. "If it isn't just-in-time, you're just out of luck," as one Y2K expert puts it.

As the year 2000 approaches, it is wise to review some of your just-in-time arrangements. If these suppliers' year 2000 efforts do not pass a stringent examination, you should consider expanding your inventory on a temporary basis, in case of a slowdown. Here, too, arranging for backup suppliers might be a good idea.

Remember that most just-in-time inventory processes work at least in part because computerization of ordering and delivery makes getting products from the supplier to your company a very efficient process. As the computers in question encounter the year 2000, that may no longer be the case.

5. **Watch out for expiration dates.** Some of the most pernicious problems that the year 2000 has already created have to do with expiration dates. Many credit card companies have so far been unable to issue cards with expiration dates of "00" or "01" because they know the card-reading machines in use at stores and restaurants would be unable to process them. Similar problems have occurred with the expiration dates on certain driver's licenses. Then there was the well-known magazine that sent out

subscription confirmation letters reading: "Your subscription is good until 1901."

That may be amusing, but if your manufacturing operation has to shut down, or your retail store computer automatically rejects perfectly good products because their expiration year begins with a zero, it won't seem so funny.

6. **Get legal protection.** Even if you believe your essential suppliers are in great shape with their year 2000 projects (and especially if you don't), you should get as much legal protection as you can. The way to do this is through a new clause in your contract with each supplier that says the supplier will be year 2000-compliant by a given date. Failing that, you could insert a clause guaranteeing that your deliverables will not be affected should the supplier encounter a year 2000 problem.

Of course, your hope is that you won't find yourself having to cite these clauses in a breach of contract suit. And, with luck, you won't. One of the best reasons for adding such a clause to your contract is that, if your suppliers have been procrastinating about dealing with the year 2000 problem, this may prompt them to take action.

The Tie-Lines That Bind

Questions of supplier compliance become much more complicated if you and they are in any sort of data transfer relationship—that is, if one or more computers at their site are connected by any sort of network to any of your computers for ease of transferring any information (such as order details) back and forth. In this case, you must not only know that they will be year 2000-compliant, you also need to be sure that their solution is one that is compatible with yours. And you need to know that their year 2000 project will be finished early enough for your two companies to thoroughly test the compatibility of your upgraded applications (with time to fix any bugs) before Y2K strikes. Again, you should consider placing the supplier under contractual obligation to get the repair completed in a compatible and timely way.

But even if you have a contract, chances are you also need a firewall. A firewall is special software that runs between your systems and the outside world and prevents certain kinds of data from getting through. Firewalls have traditionally been used to keep out viruses and illicit intruders (i.e., hackers), but the same sort of technology can also screen out noncompliant data before it "contaminates" your own. (This potential contamination is one reason the year 2000 problem has been likened to a computer virus.) Even if you're quite certain that you won't get noncompliant data from any of your suppliers, you should still consider a firewall because, in this world of rapid change and global accessibility, your staff could be networking with systems you're not even aware of.

Technology Suppliers

When it comes to companies supplying hardware, software, or materials with "embedded" computer technology (that is, items such as medical testing equipment that are not computers per se, but contain computer chips), you need much more thorough assurances. If some of the suppliers' software is due to come out in a new, year 2000-compliant version, you need to know when that version is scheduled to arrive.

External IT suppliers, like all other IT professionals, may not always meet their deadlines, however, so there should be a reasonable margin for error in their plans. If, for instance, they're planning a release date in late 1999, that probably isn't soon enough; you should proceed with your fix on the assumption that the compliant upgrade won't be available in time.

Be aware, too, that just because the new version of a program is announced and certified as year 2000-compliant, that doesn't necessarily mean that it is. Not that software suppliers are dishonest, but when upgrading a program it can be difficult to cover every single usage combination; some noncompliant data can slip through. So can other types of bugs, accidentally created in the course of a year 2000 upgrade. Keep in mind that your software supplier may be just as pressed for time, and having just as much trouble finding qualified programmers, as you are. So whatever upgrades you receive, you need time to adequately test them before your company begins using them.

Most important, you need to include year 2000 compliance language in all future contracts from now until the year 2000 is safely behind you. That language should plainly state that any new products your software or hardware suppliers deliver from here on out are guaranteed to be year 2000-compliant.

Some IT managers report that their software vendors refuse to include this in their contracts. This issue can certainly lead to difficult negotiations. But given that many programmers are still writing programs with two-digit year fields, it is a guarantee you can't afford *not* to get.

12

Hidden Benefits of Y2K

It's an ill glitch that blows nobody any good . . .

No one wants to fix the year 2000 problem. Why would they? Completing a successful year 2000 project is a huge undertaking that is horrendously expensive; that involves innumerable details and loose ends, which can easily be forgotten; and that has to be completed within a tight—and immovable—deadline. At the end of all this effort your organization will have gained nothing—except the assurance that its survival won't be threatened by an unexpected year 2000 malfunction. All in all, it seems like a pretty raw deal.

None of this is untrue. But while it can't be denied that fixing the year 2000 problem confers no direct benefit on your company (except possibly survival), there are a number of indirect benefits you can turn to your advantage once you've completed your year 2000 project. Consider the following.

✦ **Competitive advantage.** Believe it or not, if you've read this far in this book, and have taken or are about to take some steps toward your own year 2000 project, you may be way ahead of many of your competitors. Most companies that have started a year 2000 project are still in the assessment phase. And many have done nothing at all.

The good news for you, and the bad news for them, is that the year 2000 problem will not, for the most part, magically disappear in, say, 2001. Though some date calculation problems may be self-correcting over time, many others will persist. Companies that have ignored Y2K in the hope it would go away by itself will have to play catch-up for the first few years of the new millennium. Recently, an acquaintance told me about a year 2000 consultant who was gearing up his business with the specific goal of serving the post-year 2000 market. I suspect he will not lack customers.

If you have your year 2000 problem under control, your company may become an island of calm in a sea of year 2000 chaos. You can focus your attention on serving customers while your competitors are struggling to get their computers working.

✦ **Strengthened relationships with suppliers.** You cannot successfully complete a year 2000 project without close collaboration with your essential suppliers. The care you have taken to make sure they are year 2000-compliant—especially if you helped them achieve that goal—is an opportunity to deepen those relationships. Likewise, the relationships you formed with software developers and consultants who helped with Y2K will also be valuable in the future.

✦ **Strengthened relationships with customers.** If your organization's customers are other businesses, they may ask tough questions about your compliance—just as I recommended you do with your own suppliers in Chapter 11. Being able to show that you have this problem under control will solidify these relationships.

✦ **Public image.** A few months ago, I heard a rumor that a Fortune 500 company was planning a huge ad campaign around its preparedness for Y2K. At this writing, it has not yet happened, and the rumor remains unconfirmed. But beyond question, many companies (including Prudential, United Healthcare, Equifax, Cigna, and McCormick Spice, to name only a few) have taken a leadership role not only by addressing the year 2000 problem with thorough, timely, and well-planned conversion projects. They also lead by their willingness to offer these projects as examples for other companies in speeches, interviews, and presentations at year 2000 conferences.

This issue will confer more and more visibility on your company as Y2K attracts a growing degree of interest among the business and mainstream media. If yours is a field where your competitive edge is strengthened by an image as a technological leader, the benefits can be exponential.

✦ **A better software portfolio.** Capers Jones notes in his *Global Economic Impact* report (see Want to Know More?) that most companies do not really know how much software they have, or what databases they have and what they contain. Since solving the year 2000 problem means making an inventory of the software your organization owns or has licensed, you'll emerge with a much better idea of what you have—even if time constraints force you to limit your inventory to the most useful and essential programs.

If missing source code (see Chapter 2) turns out to be a problem, you will have dealt with it, either by reconverting the machine code to programming language or by giving the programs in question more modern replacements. In all likelihood, you will have also set safeguards and backups in place to prevent programming code from getting lost in the future.

Further, you'll have strengthened, deepened, and solidified your relationships with your software suppliers, and probably with the programmers and IT professionals on your staff as well. All this means that even if you did not include a single software upgrade in your year 2000 project, you'll have come out of it in a much better position to evaluate exactly what programs you have, what upgrades and improvements are feasible and desirable, and what new software to consider adding in the future.

✦ **Project management experience.** Many executives these days are taking a special interest in the concept of project management as a way to approach business problems. A year 2000 project is, among other things, a massive project management challenge. So an organization that successfully completes it cannot help but gain a tremendous amount of expertise in how to drive a project, make it work, and bring it in on time. That expertise will serve you well in every other project you take on.

Add all these advantages up and you may still think that, given the choice, you'd rather skip the year 2000 problem. Who could blame you? Regardless of what is gained from completing an effective year 2000 project, it would obviously be much easier not to start one in the first place. Few managers would choose to do this, if it wasn't a matter of life or death for their organizations.

But it is. Recognizing that fact can put you way ahead of the game if you also take timely action to deal with it.

Time is running out, but it is not too late yet to address a year 2000 problem. An organization that starts now—with a well-organized, centrally managed project that has assigned priority to mission-critical systems—should have an excellent chance of getting those systems compliant in time. That will provide a safeguard from having its basic workings, and thus its survival, threatened by a year 2000 malfunction—which is the biggest benefit of all.

How to Talk Techie: A Year 2000 Glossary

You should not need the following glossary to read this book. I've avoided technical terms wherever possible and explained them wherever it was not possible. Also, I am not including basic computer terms like "hardware" or "interface," on the assumption that most readers will be familiar with them.

Instead, this glossary defines some common terms that you may encounter if you read other works about the year 2000 problem, attend a year 2000 conference, or try to discuss this matter with technical people.

Assembler   An older computer language.
bridge   Software that allows non–year 2000 compliant systems to communicate with compliant ones. Bridges must be "built" between these two types of systems, then "burned" when the noncompliant system is brought into compliance.
C, C++   Computer languages.
client/server   A modern "architecture," in which several desktop computers are linked together by a local area network (LAN), and software used by all resides on a central file server. This technology has been replacing mainframes and midsize computers in many organizations. Though many peo-

ple assume that client/server programs are too new to contain year 2000 glitches, most of them do.

COBOL   An out-of-date computer language. Despite its obsolescence, it was once very prevalent, and there is more COBOL in use among the world's business computers than any other language. For this reason, most year 2000 repair efforts are to some extent focusing their attention on COBOL.

code   The actual words and symbols that instruct computers in programs.

compiler   A program that translates human-readable programming instructions into a machine-executable program.

compliance   The ability of software and hardware to function properly when faced with dates in or after the year 2000. Though this is a very general definition, most corporate year 2000 projects could benefit from a more specific one. For instance, does the program need to work properly in every possible situation? And how many years into the future does it need to work?

DASD   An acronym for "Direct Access Storage Device," DASD refers to any random-access storage device, such as a disk.

data expansion   Another name for field expansion.

date coding   A rarely used formula for achieving year 2000 compliance without expanding two-digit year fields to four-digit year fields. It assigns a value to every day starting with January 1, 1900—which is day 1. By this measure, January 1, 1998, is day 35,796 and January 1, 2000, is 36,526. Notice that it is possible to accurately identify dates within the current six-digit limits. But the problems and confusion this creates rarely make it worth the effort.

date field   The place in a program where a date will be inserted by a user, the computer's own calendar, or some other outside source.

distributed system   A system of individual personal computers linked together by a local area network (LAN)—as opposed to a mainframe, which is not distributed.

enterprise   IT people typically use this term to refer to an organization, or to the separate divisions or business units within that organization.

environment The type of computer and operating system on which programs run, such as the "mainframe" environment or the "client/server" environment.

event horizon The time that something begins happening. When referring to the year 2000 problem, the time when Y2K-related malfunctions will begin to occur.

field expansion Expanding programs so that two-digit date fields become four-digit date fields ("1998" instead of "98"). This is the most expensive way to solve a year 2000 problem, though it also offers the most permanent and unambiguous result.

FORTRAN An old computer language widely used in scientific and technical settings.

Hollerith card A feature of early computing. Programming instructions were hole-punched on eighty-column cards, which were then fed into the computer. Depending on how old you are, how long you've been using computers, and how good your memory is, you may remember encountering these. Avoiding the year 2000 problem (using four-digit years) with technology like this would have been prohibitively expensive and hugely inefficient.

interpretation See **windowing.**

LAN An acronym for "local area network." LANs typically link several personal computers within an organization.

legacy Older computer systems that we have inherited from the past.

logic Logic means what you think it does, but because of the way computer programs work (using logic to follow from one instruction to another and execute their given commands) this is sometimes used to refer to such things as if . . . then instructions.

logic-based See **windowing.**

migration Moving software or data from one computer system to another, often from an old, noncompliant system to a new, compliant one.

PASCAL   An older computer language.

pivot point   In **windowing**-type year 2000 solutions, the pivot point is the point at which the computer will assume a year is in the twentieth rather than the twenty-first century.

platform   Though sometimes used interchangeably with **environment,** platform refers to the type of hardware on which a program runs.

procedural   See **windowing.**

regression testing   Retesting a program after alteration (such as a year 2000 conversion) to make sure that the new adjustments have not affected its functioning.

repository   A core collection of software, usually stored in a database.

scope creep   Expanding the parameters of a project (such as adding a systems upgrade to a year 2000 conversion) to better justify its cost. Scope creep is a big problem for most year 2000 projects, which may already have trouble meeting their original goals in time to prevent malfunctions.

silver bullet   Yet-to-be-invented software that would provide a complete, foolproof, error-free solution to the entire year 2000 problem with little or no human effort. Like the yeti, the silver bullet is believed to be out there somewhere, even though there are no reliable eyewitness accounts of its existence.

source code   The instructions for a program, written by a programmer in COBOL or another computer language. Source code is then translated by a compiler into machine code, which actually drives the computer when the program runs. Missing source code presents a huge problem for year 2000 conversion efforts, since it's impossible to rewrite a program from machine code alone. Some kind of (usually costly) reconversion is needed first.

spaghetti code   A thicket of "if . . . then" and "goto" statements so tangled that it's impossible to tell where they begin and end.

test bed   A computer system that can be made to simulate an actual working environment. Programs that have been rewritten for year 2000 compliance should be tested on a test bed before they are put into actual use.

tool   A piece of software that helps programmers work on programs. There are many useful tools on the market that can help programmers make year 2000 adjustments more efficiently.

triage   The process of determining which of your systems have priority for year 2000 repairs and which can be allowed to fail without threatening your organization's survival. This term was originally used on battlefields to determine which wounded soldiers should receive scarce medical care.

UNIX   A newer, language-based operating system in use on many computers. It is particularly suited to multiuser tasks.

windows, windowing   Also called procedural, interpretation, and logic-based, this is a way of making a program year 2000-compliant without the fuss of expanding its year field from two to four digits. Instead, the programmer opens a space (or window) within the program and inserts code that determines what the first two digits of a year should be, based on its last two digits. For instance, all years with a value of 49 or less become 20XX, whereas all years with a value of 50 or more become 19XX. This is a much less expensive, though less permanent, solution than field expansion. The **pivot point** where the century changes in a windowing solution can be fixed or sliding, for instance, changing according to the current date. (This is no relation to the various Microsoft Windows products that run on personal computers.)

Want to Know More? Recommended Other Reading

1. *The Global Economic Impact of the Year 2000 Software Problem* by Capers Jones, Software Productivity Research, Inc.

   This is a 63-page white paper that explores the global impact of the year 2000, and includes such items as a country-by-country and industry-by-industry analysis of Y2K's impact. It provides an excellent broad view of the problem. You can download it at Software Productivity Research's Web page: http://www.spr.com. (To read it, you will also need to download Adobe Acrobat Reader, if you don't already have it.)

   You can also contact Software Productivity Research at:
   1 New England Executive Park, Burlington, MA 01803-5005

2. *The Year 2000 Software Crisis: Challenge of the Century* by William M. Ulrich and Ian S. Hayes, Prentice-Hall, 1997

   This book offers comprehensive, detailed information on dealing with Y2K from both a technical and a management point of view.

3. *Y2K Watch: Digital Plague Oozes Across Planet* by Charles E. Phillips and William Farrell, Morgan Stanley, March 26, 1997

This 30-page white paper is well written and fun, contains some comments from programmers who helped create the year 2000 problem, and gives a great overview of the problem, as well as some predictions of which vendors are likely to be good investments. It is available from Morgan Stanley & Co.

4. *Year/2000 Journal* published by Marbo Enterprises, Inc., PO Box 550547, Dallas, TX 75355-0547   (214) 349-2147 fax: (214) 341-7081, e-mail: y2kjournal@connect.net.

As this briefing went to press, this quarterly journal had just published its first issue, which was full of interesting articles and helpful information on various aspects of the year 2000 problem. Most (though not all) could be easily understood by nontechnical readers. Short "sidebar" comments from corporate executives at work on Y2K were particularly interesting.

5. *Managing 00: Surviving the Year 2000 Computing Crisis* by Peter de Jager and Richard Bergeon, John Wiley & Sons, 1997

A fun and friendly book, it gives advice on addressing the year 2000 problem within your organization, as well as information on the various types of software tools available.

Useful World Wide Web pages:

Year 2000 issues are constantly changing, and one of the best ways to keep track of them is by checking in with some of the Web pages devoted to this issue. Here are a few of the best:

http://www.year2000.com

This is Peter de Jager's Web site. It contains links to many useful writings by de Jager and other Y2K experts, job listings, and a general forum on the subject.

http://www.y2k-info.com

The Year 2000 Information Line, it offers an index of articles that you can hear by calling a 900 number. There are also many links to other informative pages.

http://www.itaa.com

This is the Information Technology Association of America's home page.

http://www.spr.com

This is Software Productivity Research's home page.

http://www.wsrcg.com

This is consultant Warren S. Reid's home page. It includes useful articles on the year 2000 problem.

About the Author

Minda Zetlin is a freelance writer who specializes in business management and technology. She is a regular contributor to the AMA magazine *Management Review,* as well as *Nation's Business, Cosmopolitan, Games,* and many others. She also covers technology in emerging markets for the IBM Web magazine *Other Voices.* E-mail her at MindaZ@aol.com or visit her web site at http://members.aol.com/MindaZ.

She lives in Woodstock, New York.

OTHER MANAGEMENT BRIEFINGS OF INTEREST

MANAGEMENT BRIEFING ORDER FORM

(A multiple-copy discount is available. Call for details.)

Please send me the following:

☐ ＿＿ copies of **A Better Place to Work: A New Sense of Motivation Leading to Higher Productivity,** Stock #2363XMLL, $17.95/$16.15 AMA Members.

☐ ＿＿ copies of **Beyond Customer Satisfaction to Customer Loyalty: The Key to Greater Profitability,** Stock #2362XMLL, $19.95/$17.95 AMA Members.

☐ ＿＿ copies of **The New OSHA: A Blueprint for Effective Training and Written Programs,** Stock #2360XMLL, $24.95/$22.45 AMA Members.

☐ ＿＿ copies of **The Management Compass: Steering the Corporation Using Hoshin Planning,** Stock #2358XMLL, $19.95/$17.95 AMA Members.

☐ ＿＿ copies of **Mentoring: Helping Employees Reach Their Full Potential,** Stock #2357XMLL, $14.95/$13.45 AMA Members.

☐ ＿＿ copies of **Blueprints for Service Quality: The Federal Express Approach, SECOND EDITION,** Stock #2356XMLL, $14.95/$13.45 AMA Members.

Name: ＿＿＿＿＿＿＿＿＿＿＿＿＿＿＿＿＿＿＿＿＿＿＿＿＿＿＿

Title: ＿＿＿＿＿＿＿＿＿＿＿＿＿＿＿＿＿＿＿＿＿＿＿＿＿＿＿＿

Organization: ＿＿＿＿＿＿＿＿＿＿＿＿＿＿＿＿＿＿＿＿＿＿＿＿

Street Address: ＿＿＿＿＿＿＿＿＿＿＿＿＿＿＿＿＿＿＿＿＿＿＿

City, State, Zip: ＿＿＿＿＿＿＿＿＿＿＿＿＿＿＿＿＿＿＿＿＿＿＿

Phone: (＿＿＿) ＿＿＿＿＿＿＿＿＿ FAX: (＿＿＿) ＿＿＿＿＿＿＿

Applicable sales tax and shipping & handling will be added.

☐ Charge my credit card ☐ Bill me ☐ AMA Member

Card # ＿＿＿＿＿＿＿＿＿＿＿＿＿＿＿ Exp. Date ＿＿＿＿＿＿＿

Signature: ＿＿＿＿＿＿＿＿＿＿＿＿＿＿＿＿＿＿＿＿＿＿＿＿＿＿

Purchase Order #: ＿＿＿＿＿＿＿＿＿＿＿＿＿＿＿＿＿＿＿＿＿＿

AMA'S NO-RISK GUARANTEE: If for any reason you are not satisfied, we will credit the purchase price toward another product or refund your money. **No hassles. No loopholes. Just excellent service. That is what AMA is all about.**

Management Briefings
AMA Publication Services
P.O. Box 319
Saranac Lake, NY 12983

Visit our website: www.amanet.org